QUESTIONS AND EXERCISES

IN

ELEMENTARY LOGIC

DEDUCTIVE AND INDUCTIVE

1875

PREFACE.

IN PUTTING FORTH this little work, the intention of the Editor has been to keep in view the original design of the *Palæstra Oxoniensis*; viz. to give a selection of questions in the various subjects which have from time to time been set in the Schools.

As in Logic the student meets with most of his difficulties in the earlier part of his studies, the particular object of this book has been to avoid as much as possible the multiplicity of technical terms, and to explain those points which are but slightly noticed in more advanced works on the same subject. It is not intended to supersede any text-book now in existence, but rather to be a supplement to them; for it is believed that the careful use of questions will lead to a thorough knowledge of this subject.

OXFORD: *August* 1875.

CONTENTS.

INTRODUCTORY:
                PAGE
  SECTION I. Definition of Logic 1
   „ II. Perception, Imagination, Sensation . 4
   „ III. Main Divisions of Logic . . . 4
   „ IV. Use of Logic 5

DEDUCTIVE.

TERMS.

CHAPTER
 I. THE VARIOUS KINDS OF TERMS . . . 7
 II. ON DENOTATION AND CONNOTATION OF TERMS 10

PROPOSITIONS.

 III. DIVISION OF PROPOSITIONS 14
 IV. DISTRIBUTION OF TERMS 19
 V. PREDICABLES 20
 VI. DEFINITION 23
 VII. DIVISION 26

INFERENCES.

CHAPTER		PAGE
VIII.	OF INFERENCE	29
IX.	OPPOSITION	30
X.	CONVERSION	33
XI.	SYLLOGISMS	37
	SECTION I. Of the Nature of Syllogisms	39
	” II. Moods	41
	” III. Syllogistic Rules	42
	” IV. Figures	46
	” V. Special Rules for Figures	48
	” VI. Syllogism with two Particular Premisses	51
	” VII. Reduction	51
XII.	THE ENTHYMEME, SORITES, INDUCTION, ANALOGY, AND EXAMPLE	56
XIII.	COMPLEX OR HYPOTHETICAL SYLLOGISMS AND DILEMMA	61–66
XIV.	FALLACIES	67
	SECTION I. Fallacies in dictione	69
	” II. Fallacies extra dictionem	71
	” III. Exercises on Fallacies	74
XV.	METHOD	79

INDUCTIVE.

XVI.	INDUCTION	81
XVII.	OBSERVATION AND EXPERIMENT	86

Contents.

CHAPTER		PAGE
XVIII.	METHODS OF INDUCTION	88
	SECTION I. Cause and Effect	89
	,, II. First Canon. (Method of Agreement)	90
	,, III. Second Canon. (Method of Difference)	91
	,, IV. Third Canon. (Joint Method of Agreement and Difference)	92
	,, V. Fourth Canon. (Method of Residues)	93
	,, VI. Fifth Canon. (Method of Concomitant Variations)	93
XIX.	HYPOTHESIS	94
XX.	PROBABLE REASONING	97
INDEX OF LOGICAL TERMS		99

QUESTIONS AND EXERCISES IN
ELEMENTARY LOGIC.

INTRODUCTORY.

GIVE *all the definitions of Logic you know, and your opinion of them.*

Is it in its capacity of an Art or a Science that Logic is a branch of Psychology?

Explain precisely the grounds on which Logic is called both a Science and an Art.

Logic has been called 'Ars Artium.' In what sense is the term applicable to it?

What is your conception of Logic? For what purposes do you consider its study useful?

'People can reason without the help of Logic.' Is this a conclusive argument against the utility of Logic?

Compare Logic, Rhetoric, and Grammar. What are the faults of the following definitions of Logic: Logic is a mental science; Logic is the art of expressing thought in words; Logic is a help to correct reasoning.

SECTION I.

Psychology is a science which treats of the various **phenomena** connected with the mind. Such are Sensation, Imagination, Perception, Volition, Conception, Reflection, &c. Thus we see that it extends over a very wide field of subjects; whereas Logic is only a branch of psychology, for it only treats of that intellectual part of the mind which is concerned with reflection or thought; and it is, of course, rather in its capacity of a science that Logic is connected with psychology.

Now Logic has been variously defined by all classes of writers from the earliest times;[1] but it will be sufficient for us to examine a few of the more prominent definitions.

Archbishop Whateley, to whom is due the revival of the study, defined Logic to be 'the science and art of reasoning.' This was an old definition, except that he put in the word 'art;' and it seems too narrow. Logic, he said, was exclusively concerned with language, and principally with argumentation in language. Thus he excluded from the study everything that treated of terms and propositions, except so far as it was subservient to reasoning. The definition given by Mr. Mill, on the other hand, seems too wide: 'Logic is the science of the operations of the understanding, which are subservient to the laws of evidence.' This would make Logic depend on experience, and regards more the matter than the form of argumentation: 'it includes within the province of Logic processes governed by different laws, involving fundamentally different methods.'[2]

Another definition is, that 'Logic is the science of the formal laws of thought.' This is the one adopted by Mansel, who follows more or less the Aristotelian

[1] Vide Mansel's 'Aldrich,' Introduction, p. 58.
[2] See Mansel's Introduction to 'Aldrich.'

principles, and those of the Schoolmen. But here, again, the definition seems to be insufficient. Logic is not only the science of the laws of thought, by which we distinguish what correct thoughts are; it extends farther than this. It not only investigates what thought and reasoning is, but it supplies us with rules by which we may attain to correct thoughts; and in the former case it is a science, in the latter case an art.

It is true that it is possible to reason without Logic. So also can we eat without a knife and fork; so also can we dye a garment without a knowledge of chemistry; but this does not take away from the value of the science as leading to the practice of the art. It is possible to be proficient in a science without being able to practise the art; it is possible to practise the art without any scientific knowledge. But if we know both, we shall do better than those who only know one or other. Therefore we can reason without the use of Logic, as the majority do; but the very mistakes of the majority prove the usefulness of Logic.

But what Logic really does is to sit in judgment on the rules, and test the method of the other sciences. It is the guide of the intellect, which is used necessarily in all other sciences and arts; and it is in this sense that it may be called 'Scientia Scientiarum,' and 'Ars Artium;' it is in this sense that it is the master science.

It has been doubted by some logicians whether we can or cannot think without language; but as a matter of fact we never do, and certainly we cannot communicate our thoughts without language; but still, in Logic, language is only a secondary object; and in this, Logic differs from grammar, in which language is the primary object. The grammarian interests himself with the forms of words and the construction of sentences, whereas the logician only desires to find out and test the thoughts which the sentences express.

Logic again differs from Rhetoric, in that it is the art of conviction, Rhetoric the art of persuasion. Logic appeals to the head, Rhetoric to the heart. Logic only deals with truth, Rhetoric often finds much power in falsehood.

SECTION II.

Distinguish Perception, Imagination, Sensation.

These three are intuitive faculties, and have nothing to do with Thought. Sensation is a consciousness of external impressions brought about through an organ of sense[1]—a physical effect on the *sensorium*.

Perception is the apprehension of something before our eyes—a mental effect: *e.g.* I can perceive the inkstand before me, its shape, its form, its size.

Imagination, on the other hand, is the operation of recalling to mind some absent object: *e.g.* To-morrow, when out of my study, I can recall to my mind the shape, form, and size of the inkstand on my table.[2]

SECTION III.

What are the three main divisions of Logic? Under which—and for what reasons—would you place the discussion of Predicables, Opposition, Conversion, Definition, and Division?

Into what parts is Logic usually divided? What is the proper business of each part?

'Mentis operationes in universum tres sunt. More

---

[1] Vide Carpenter's 'Mental Physiology,' bk. i. ch. iv.
[2] For Constructive and Creative Imagination, &c., see Carpenter's 'Mental Physiology,' bk. ii. ch. xii.

correctly, the products of pure thought are three: the Concept, the Judgment, and the Syllogism.'[1]

This is the opinion of those who look upon Logic as dealing with pure Thought: those who look upon it as dealing with Language, call the three parts of Logic Terms, Propositions, and Inferences. Mr. Mill, again, says that Logic treats of the objects themselves concerning which we argue. But in any case Logic is separated into three main divisions; and though logicians use different expressions, they all more or less mean the same thing. The Term is the Concept expressed in words; the Proposition is the Judgment, and so on.

The discussion of the Heads of Predicables determines the place of Definition and Division. Opposition and Conversion come under the second or third part, according as they are looked upon as propositions only, or inferences.[2]

Section IV.

'*Each operation of the mind has its own defect.*' *How do the rules of Logic remedy these defects?*

How far does Logic conduce to clearness of thought, and accuracy of statement?

Keeping before us the definition that Logic is both an art and a science—a science in that it investigates what thought is, art in that it supplies rules for practice —we can see that every one of its rules is calculated to remedy defects in our thoughts, and consequently at the same time to cause us to state those thoughts with accuracy. We often hear the expression, 'I know what I mean, but cannot express myself.' It is exactly to

[1] Mansel's 'Aldrich.'
[2] See Mr. Fowler's 'Logic,' Part ii. ch. v., note 1, where the question is answered.

remedy this difficulty that Logic is useful. The fault of the first part of Logic is Indistinctness. The rules for the Definition and Division of Terms will prevent this. They both teach us to know how much we mean by a term; how many qualities the said term possesses, which distinguish it from other terms; how many individuals are denoted by it; and by these means therefore we are enabled to attain to correct thoughts, and also to express them in accurate language.

The fault of the second operation is Falsity of Judgment. This we may detect by the rules of Opposition and Conversion, the value of which consists in the fact that they evolve all that is involved in a statement. If we say, 'All men are mortal,' by conversion we learn that we do not mean to deny mortality of other things than men, but that men belong to the class of things called mortal. Thus, by the rules of conversion, we cannot say, 'All mortal things are men,' and so we learn *how much* we meant by the first statement, 'All men are mortal.'

Again, from the laws of Opposition, we learn that Contradictories cannot be true together, or false together; and if we state what is true, 'All men are mortal,' we *know* that its contradictory, 'Some men are not mortal,' is false. Thus we know the exact grounds on which we take our stand, and are careful to state those grounds with accuracy. The fault of the third part—False Inference—is to be detected by the rules of syllogistic reasoning. The consideration of them is too long to be entered into here, but they will be taken in detail in later answers.

TERMS.

CHAPTER I.

THE VARIOUS KINDS OF TERMS.

GIVE the Definition and principal Divisions of the Term in Logic.

Define Collective, Relative, Syncategorematic, Common, Infinite, Equivocal Terms.

What is a noun of Second Intention? Classify terms. What are Concrete Terms, and what is their relation to your classification?

Explain Singular, Collective, and Common Terms, giving instances of each class. Explain Infinite Term: what is its use? To what heads would you refer the following terms respectively:—heat, light, the sun, temperance, the Athenians, gold, metal, the navy, the clergy, parent, home, essay, truth, legion?

Distinguish Nomina Relativa and Nomina Repugnantia. Assign the following to one or other class:—Hope, Fear; Right, Left; All, None; Concave, Convex; Great, Small.

What kinds of words can stand as the subject of a Proposition, and what kinds are excluded?

The first part of Logic treats of Simple Terms, which are made up of words or numbers of words; and words have been divided into two great classes—Categorematic, or those which can stand by themselves as predicate of a proposition, and are complete terms; and Syncategorematic, or those which cannot so stand, but must have other words *with* them to make them complete terms.

Thus Logic only recognises the noun and the verb as its parts of speech, and not all of those parts; for nouns in the oblique cases, and verbs in the past or future tenses, together with participles, adjectives, adverbs, prepositions, &c., are syncategorematic.

A Term is the boundary of a Proposition, *i.e.* either its subject or predicate, and may consist of one word or many together, expressing one notion. Thus, 'horse,' 'man,' 'man-going-down-the-street,' 'the-man-dressed-in-a-green-coat,' are all terms.

But beside this main division of terms, there are many distinctions to be noticed.

I. Terms are Singular, and General or Common. Singular terms are those which refer to a single individual object, as Socrates, the sun, the Czar. General or Common terms are those which can be applied equally to many objects, whether taken separately or together; *e.g.* 'man' may apply to one man, or to the whole human race. There is another kind of term which may be applied to a number of individual objects, but only when they are taken together or collectively. These are Collective terms; *e.g.* legion, the clergy, the House of Commons.

II. Again, distinguish the concrete and abstract term. Mr. Mill says, concrete terms are the names of things, abstract terms are the names of the attributes of things. Thus white house is the name of a thing, and is *concrete*; whiteness is the quality or attribute which belongs to the thing, and is *abstract*. We may here notice that singular, collective, and common terms, as well as adjective, are concrete.

III. There is again a distinction between positive and negative terms. Positive terms imply the possession or existence of some quality, the negative term implies its absence; *e.g.* grateful and ungrateful. Another kind of negative is called the privative term, which implies the absence of a quality from an object which might have had it; *e.g. blind*, as applied to man, is privative, as he once was capable of seeing; for even if born *blind*, he had the organs of sight: *blind* as applied to a stone is negative, as it never could have seen.[1]

IV. There is again another distinction between Relative and Absolute or Non-relative terms. Relative terms are those where we cannot think of one object without reference to some other object. Thus 'parent' at once implies 'child,' 'guardian' implies 'ward,' 'master' implies 'servant;' and, as Socrates says, 'thirst' implies 'drink.'

V. Another and most important distinction is that between Univocal, Equivocal, and Analogous terms. Univocal terms are those which are only used in one sense, and never ambiguously, *i.e.* in more than one sense; Equivocal and Analogous terms are those which are ambiguous. Equivocal terms are those with which people make puns; *e.g.* Hood says,—

> The love that loves a scarlet coat
> Should be more uniform.

These often arise from a difference of derivation, or a transfer of meaning. Sometimes a term is used ambiguously from analogy or resemblance. Thus 'foot' is the basis of a thing; we, from the analogy of the foot of a man, get 'the foot of a mountain.'

---

[1] Mr. Mansel says this is a bad division of Aldrich. 'Negative nouns should not be contrasted with positive, but with affirmative, and belong to another kind of opposition, the contradictory. Opposition of terms is fourfold. 1. Relative,—father and son; 2. Contrary,—black and white; 3. Privative,—blind and seeing; 4. Contradictory,—man and not man. This last of all is also called an Infinite term, and is useful in all parts of logic where Dichotomy by Contradiction is used.

This distinction is most important, because so many fallacies arise from the use of ambiguous terms.

VI. The old logicians make another distinction between Nouns of First Intention and Nouns of Second Intention.

A noun of the first intention is a word in common use; as man, animal, &c. A noun of the second intention is a technical logical word. This definition given by Aldrich is somewhat vague; but Mr. Mansel quotes Hobbes on this point. 'Of the *first intention* are the names of things, as *man, stone*, &c.; of the *second* are the [names of names, and speeches, as *universal, particular, genus, species, syllogism*, and the like.' A first intention is a conception under which the mind regards things; a second intention is 'a conception under which the mind regards its first intentions as related to each other.' Thus the relation of *animal* to *man*, or *man* to *animal*, is as a *genus* or a *species*; and the latter words are nouns of *second intention*.

CHAPTER II.

ON DENOTATION AND CONNOTATION OF TERMS.

What is meant by Denotation and Connotation? What logical processes are meant to give them exactness?

'In a series of common terms, standing to each other in the relation of subordination, the denotation and connotation vary inversely.' Explain this.

Distinguish between the Denotation and Connotation of Terms.

Explain the distinction implied in the terms Intension and Extension. In what other manner has it been expressed?
'The greater the Connotation of a term the less its Denotation.' Explain this.[1]

A term is denotative when it designates or points out an individual or group of individuals: it is connotative when it denotes the subject, and connotes the attributes. A non-connotative name is one which denotes a subject only, or attribute only. This is the distinction given by Mr. Mill, who is supposed to be the best authority on this subject; but it is different from the views of many others. All general concrete terms are connotative, as well as denotative; thus *man* denotes a number of individuals, and at the same time connotes a number of attributes, which belong to the individuals in virtue of which they are called by one common name. Abstract terms, being the names only of attributes, would as a rule, according to Mr. Mill, be non-connotative; but some might be connotative, viz. such as implied the attributes of attributes, *e.g.* virtue connotes fortitude, temperance, &c. But proper names are non-connotative, as also are singular and collective names; because, though they denote individuals, they do not at the same time directly imply any attributes of those individuals.[2]

The Denotation and Connotation of a term has been otherwise expressed as the Extension and Intension or comprehension of a term. The extension implies all the objects or *individuals* contained in the term, the

---

[1] These two last are one and the same question.
[2] On the whole subject, see Mill's 'Logic,' bk. i. ch. ii.; and Jevons, Lesson V.

intension implies all the *qualities* possessed by the individuals contained in the term. There is a general rule by which the extensive and intensive capacity of a term is determined, and this is as follows—'*the greater the extension or denotation, the less the intension or connotation.*' This we shall see from the following diagram, called *Arbor Porphyriana*.

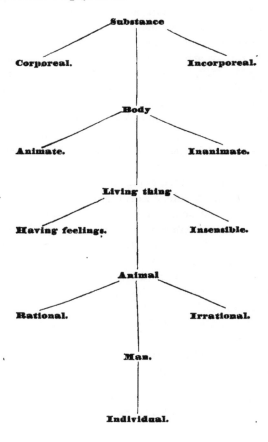

Here the common terms Substance, Body, Living Thing, Animal, Man, 'stand to one another in the relation of subordination,' and we shall find that the bottom one is most intensive, and the top one most extensive; for if we take man and animal, the word man denotes or extends over a very much smaller number of objects than animal; but we know more about the attributes of man than we do about those of animals. Again, if we go higher, from animal to living thing, we get a larger group of objects—we now include the vegetable as well as the animal world—but our knowledge of the attributes is still less; and so on, if we go higher, the terms get more extensive, but less intensive; but on the other hand, as we come down the terms get more intensive, and less extensive. This is what is meant by saying that the denotation and connotation vary inversely.[1]

[1] The Arbor Porphyriana is used for another purpose in logic, viz. for an explanation of the predicables. It is inserted here as an illustration only.

PROPOSITIONS.

CHAPTER III.
DIVISION OF PROPOSITIONS.

WHAT are the forms, and how designated, of Logical Propositions? In what way, and with what object, has a modern philosopher proposed to innovate on these forms?

What is a Modal Proposition? How may Modal Propositions be expressed in a pure logical form? [1]

Distinguish Verbal and Real Proposition.

What do you mean by the Quantity and Quality of a Proposition?

Explain Copula, Predicate, Modality, Proposition. Propositio Singularis æque potest Universali. Explain this.

The Proposition, which is treated of in the second part of Logic, may be said to be a Judgment expressed in words. It arises from comparison. We think of two terms, and then compare them with each other, and we state the result of our comparison in a proposition. Thus we think of horse, and black; and as the terms agree or differ we say, 'the horse is black,' or 'the horse is-not black.' 'The-man-going-down-the-street-with-a-green-coat-on, is (or 'is-not,' as the case may be) a Forester.' Here it is plain that a proposition consists of three parts: viz. the two terms compared, and the affirmative or negative verb, which connects them. This connecting link—'is' or 'is-not'—is called the Copula;

---
[1] Fowler, p. 26.

and here notice that the copula expresses *merely affirmation or negation* : it cannot express time, place, manner, or existence. All propositions expressing these must be first reduced to logical form before they can be treated in a logical way.[1]

The other two parts of the proposition are called the *subject* and *predicate*. The subject is that term *of which* the other is asserted or denied ; *e.g.* in the above examples 'the horse,' 'the man-going,' &c., and the predicate is *that which is* asserted or denied, *e.g.* 'black,' 'a Forester.'

Propositions are divided, according to substance, into Categorical and Hypothetical. Categorical are subdivided into pure and modal ; hypothetical into conjunctive, disjunctive, &c.[2] Taking then Categoricals, modal propositions may be dismissed in a few words. 'Aristotle mentions four modes, the *necessary*, the *impossible*, the *contingent*, and the *possible*. Later logicians have multiplied the number. . . . Any adverb annexed to the predicate was regarded as forming a modal,' according to Mansel.[3] These, however, seem to be out of the province of Formal Logic.

Categoricals, then, are divided according to their *quality* or *quantity*. They are divided according to *quality* into Affirmative and Negative. An affirmative, as will be seen from what has been said of the predicate, asserts that some of the qualities, or all, in the predicate belong to the subject ; *e.g.* (to keep an old and easy illustration) the proposition 'All men are mortal' asserts that the quality of mortality belongs to men. The negative proposition denies that the qualities indi-

[1] See note, and exercises at the end of this section.
[2] Hypothetical propositions will be discussed later on.
[3] Mansel's 'Aldrich.'

cated by the predicate belong to the subject; 'the horse is not black' shows that the quality of blackness does not belong to the horse; 'no bats are birds' denies that the qualities which belong to birds belong to bats also.

Propositions are divided as to *quantity* into universal, particular, Indefinite and Singular. Singular propositions may be treated as universals, as, *e.g.* Socrates is a philosopher, means that the whole subject 'Socrates'—all we know of him—is a philosopher: indefinite propositions are extra-logical, as we must apply to experience to find out *how much* we mean to assert, *e.g.* '*most* men have waistcoats' does not indicate how many have. Thus there are left Universal and Particular propositions. Universal propositions are those which assert or deny the predicate as belonging to the whole of the subject; as 'All men are mortal,' 'All bats are not birds.'[1] Particular propositions are those which do not assert or deny the predicate of the whole of the subject.

As there are, then, Affirmatives, Negatives, Particulars, and Universals, it is easy to see that there are four kinds of propositions :—

Universal Affirmative . . . . A.
Universal Negative . . . . E.
Particular Affirmative . . . . I.
Particular Negative . . . . O.

These are designated, for convenience sake, in works on Logic, by the first four vowels of the alphabet, in capital letters.

The distinction between Verbal and Real propositions may be stated as follows: A verbal proposition tells us

---

[1] Here notice, 'all' must be taken in a distributive sense. All the jury are twelve (taken collectively), is a singular proposition.

in the predicate nothing new about the subject; but a real proposition does. These are also called Analytical and Synthetical judgments.[1]

Quantification of the Predicate. Sir W. Hamilton, with a view to reducing all propositions to the same quantity, simplifying conversion and omitting distribution of terms, introduced a plan to innovate on the old forms of proposition, viz. always to mark the quantity of the predicate.[2] The whole amounts to this : 'Does the whole predicate, or only a part of it, agree with or differ from the subject?'

It is as well to state here, that the student must not always expect to find propositions stated in the proper logical form, and therefore a careful analysis of each proposition is always useful. The subject, predicate, and copula should always be carefully sought for, and when found should be accurately stated. It is recommended that the copula should be separated from the others by perpendicular lines, thus :—

The horse | is | black :

and in each exercise that the words, Subject, Copula, Predicate, should be written over the parts of the proposition, as below :—

Sub.   *Cop.*   *Predicate.*
The horse | is | black.

It may seem trouble at first, but it leads to an accurate knowledge of the work. Thus, 'All that glitters is not gold,' must first be put into logical form. What does it mean? Not 'all' glittering things, but only ' some :' thus we get—

[1] See Mansel's 'Aldrich,' Appendix A.
[2] For a full account, see Jevons, Less. xxii.

Some things that glitter | are not | gold.

Again, 'None but the brave deserve the fair;' here 'none but' evidently means 'none who are not,' thus

None who are not brave | are | deserving of the fair.

Some exercises are here given for the help of the patient student :—

EXERCISES.

Arrange the following according to Quality and Quantity, and put them into Logical Propositions.

He can't be wrong, whose life is in the right.
All, save the spirit of man, is divine.
'T is use alone that sanctifies expense.
It is probable that the standard both of reason and taste is the same in all human creatures.
The most advanced Reformer would not dream of discontinuing the Lord Mayor's dinner.
You all look strangely on me.
Man made the town.
Dead men tell no tales.
Non omnis moriar.
What I have written, I have written.
A man's a man for a' that.
He jests at scars who never felt a wound.
The proper study of mankind is man.
One touch of nature makes the whole world kin.
'T is only noble to be good.
Mercy but murders, pardoning those who kill.
It is not everyone who can understand treatises on Logic.[1]

[1] All these examples will be useful for Conversion also.

CHAPTER IV.

DISTRIBUTION OF TERMS.

WHAT do you mean by Distribution of Terms? How is it useful for testing the value of the syllogism?

Give and prove the rules for the Distribution of Terms, and show their use in Logic.

What are the rules for the distribution of terms, and their exceptions?

Why do negatives distribute their predicate? Do affirmatives ever distribute theirs?

The rules for the distribution of terms are two:—

1st. Universals, and Universals *only*, distribute their subject.

2nd. Negatives, and Negatives *only*, distribute their predicate.

A term is distributed *when taken in its widest extent*. In the proposition, 'All swans are white,' it is asserted that whiteness is a quality of *every thing* that we can think of that comes under the term swan. Thus swan is distributed.

'No men are angels' denies every possible quality of angel to every possible individual man; thus both 'angel' and 'man' are taken in their widest extent, and are distributed. 'Some men are wise' distributes neither 'men' nor 'wise.' '*Some* men' evidently is not taken in the widest extent, and we cannot say that 'all wisdom' belongs to 'some men'; here, then, neither of the terms are distributed. But if we say, 'Some men are not wise,' we deny everything in the way of wisdom (distributed) of some men. Thus we have examined the four propositions, A, E, I, O, and

    A distributes its subject.
    E   „   its subject and predicate.
    I   „   neither.
    O   „   its predicate.[1]

CHAPTER V.

PREDICABLES.

Name the five Heads of Predicables.

In the operations of natural science, which of these heads holds the most prominent place?

In what different relations may a subject and predicate stand to one another? Give instances.

Define Predicable. Distinguish Differentia and Property—Separable and Inseparable Accident.

In what do Differentia, Property, and Accident differ from each other?

Define Predicable: give the Genus, Differentia, Property, and Accident, where ' money' is the subject.

In each of the following sentences point out the predicate, and refer it to the head of predicables to which it belongs:—

    (1.) *Alkalies by their union with acids form salts.*
    (2.) *The tiger is a predatory animal.*
    (3.) *Some governments rest upon force.*

These rules should be carefully learnt for future use. Distribution ms is most important in the syllogism, as will be seen, when we state les.

(4.) *James ruled oppressively.*
(5.) *All equilateral triangles are equiangular.*
(6.) *All triangles in their angles contain two right angles.*

Genus, Species, Differentia, Property, Accident—these are the five heads of Predicables, and they are so called because it is in one of these five ways that a subject stands in relation to the predicate of a proposition, and sometimes in more than one at the same time. For instance, in 'All men are mortal,' the subject stands in the relation of *species* to *genus*; in 'men are rational' it is a relation of species, and differentia; in 'Socrates is a philosopher,' it is a relation of individual to a species, and so on. It will be necessary to explain each of these five heads of predicables.

If the reader will turn back to the tree of Porphyry, he will see that the various terms are subordinate to each other, and will understand what is meant by a *genus*, by taking any one of the terms, and considering it in its relation to the one below. Thus 'substance' is the genus of 'body'; 'body' of 'living thing,' and so on, as we go down. Thus we see, then, that genus is a class, which contains other classes under it. Again, this class, which is contained in the genus, is called a *species*, with reference to the genus: and as we go up the tree, we see that we go from species to genus. Thus 'man' is a species of 'animal,' 'animal' of 'living thing,' and so on. Species, then, is the name of a class, which is contained under some wider class or genus. 'Substance' is said to be the Summum Genus, because it has no genus above it; and 'Man' is said to be the Infima Species, as it has no species below it; for individuals are not species: the intermediate terms are subaltern Genera and Species.

If we look again to the tree, we see certain words on the left hand, such as corporeal, animate, having feeling, rational. These are called differences, or *differentiæ*, because they distinguish some individuals of a class from all others under that same class: *e.g.* 'rational' distinguishes man from all other animals; 'animate' distinguishes living beings from all other kinds of bodies. It will from this be easy to see that if the difference is added to the genus, we get the species; thus the genus *plus* the differentia is said *to constitute the species.*

The next predicable is *Property*; and this is most difficult to describe, as there is much difference of opinion among logicians about it. It seems best to say that it is an attribute belonging to all the members of a class, but does not always distinguish that class from others under the same genus. Mr. Mill's definition is that 'property is an attribute, which belongs to all the individuals included in a species, and which, though not connoted by the specific name, yet follows from some attribute which the name either ordinarily or specially connotes.' Thus we speak of 'laughter' as a property of man; also 'memory,' and the like—which are all more or less dependent on a man's rationality. At any rate, a property is something *peculiar* (ἴδιον) to the members of a class; and it approaches very closely sometimes to a differentia.

We have *Accident* still left to consider. 'The rhinoceros is an animal, *that lives in the Zoological Gardens.*' 'Man is an animal, *that plays on the fiddle.*' Here we can see plainly that the words in italics indicate an accident: they are not part of the connotation of either the term 'man' or 'rhinoceros.' Thus an accident may y not belong to a term: it belongs to it *by chance*, ntally.

Accidents are separable and inseparable, and belong to a class or an individual. Inseparable accidents of a class are those attributes which we find always belonging to a class, whose absence, however, would not affect the class, as 'All crows are black.' Separable accidents of a class are those attributes which are sometimes applied and sometimes not, as 'Some horses are black.'

Inseparable accidents of the Individual are those from which he can never escape—'John Robinson was born in Paris;' 'Smith has red hair.'

Separable accidents may not always be present— 'Smith is sitting down;' 'Robinson is playing the fiddle.'[1]

CHAPTER VI.

DEFINITION.

STATE the object, method, and use of Definition.

What are the rules and difficulties of Definition?

Explain, with examples, the various forms of Definition.

What is a Definition: when is it valid, and to what defects is it liable?

What are the conditions of a good Definition? Give instances of their violation.

What is the nature and use of Definition?

[1] The student should read Mansel's Appendix A, to 'Aldrich's Logic,' as well as the notes, for a full account of Predicables.

Definition is the explanation of the meaning of a term : it therefore is limited to those terms which have a meaning. In other words, it is 'the exposition of the connotation of a term' (*Fowler*), and those words which have no connotation cannot be accurately defined. Thus proper names, singular, and collective terms, cannot be defined, but only described. Thus at the outset we see that there are many terms which cannot be defined. The best definition is said to be that which we gain *per genus et differentiam*. But to guide us to a good definition there are three rules—

1. The definition must be adequate to the thing defined ; that is, it must contain neither more nor less than the thing defined. Thus, 'house is a building' is not adequate ; the word 'building' contains more than the thing defined, for there are many buildings which are not houses.

2. The definition must be *per se* clearer and better known than the thing defined ; *i.e.* it must be greater in extension, and better known, for it would be useless to attempt to give the meaning of a thing by describing something less known than itself—*ignotum per ignotius*.

3. The definition must be expressed in words in common use.[1]

From this we can see the difficulties of good definition : in all cases it is hard, in some impossible, to comply with the above rules. The definition *per genus et differentiam*, however, will be most satisfactory : in other cases we must keep to the rules as closely as possible. In cases where our knowledge is fixed and certain, we are able to give a perfect definition ; but where our knowledge is only progressing, the definition must be provisional. Thus in sciences, which are at present only partially known, we must be satisfied with provisional definitions. Again, we may have a special purpose in hand; then we may make an apparent definition, suited for that purpose, *e.g.* 'Man is a bartering animal' is sufficient for political economy to distinguish man from other animals. Cuvier's description, 'Man is a mammiferous animal with two hands' was sufficient for his purpose in natural history. These are properly *descriptions*, but are comparatively complete; whereas others are much more vague, *e.g.* 'the lion is the king of beasts' is no definition at all, and scarcely a description, for it does not in any way serve to distinguish the lion from other beasts, save in the matter of strength, which the word 'king' means; and many other beasts are per chance as strong as the lion.

Definition is most useful for making us think accurately: by it we are enabled to know clearly what a term means, so that we need never use such term in any vague or doubtful sense; and thus it is possible always clearly to understand what we are thinking about: accuracy of statement must follow from clearness of thought; but Definition regards terms rather than propositions.

The student is advised in the following exercises to keep as closely as possible to the rules before mentioned, and give the genus and difference; and to follow the same plan in testing the definitions here given:—

Define—*Lightning, Emulation, Riot, Committee, Garden, Honour, Revenge, Franchise, Library, House, School, College, Minister, Governor, Hypocrisy, Treason, Logic, Syllogism, University, Club, Dictionary, Hypochondria* (1867), *Race-horse, Insurance, Parent, Nation, Monarchy, Courage.*

Examine the following definitions, and show their defects, if any :—

Lion—the fiercest and most magnanimous of beasts.

Jockey—a fellow that rides in a race.
Chest—a box of wood or other materials in which things are laid up.
Stork—a bird of passage, famous for the regularity of its departure.
Rust—the red desquamation of old iron.
Biscuit—a kind of hard bread made to be carried to sea.
Man—a biped without feathers.
Cheese—a caseous preparation of milk.
Liquid—that which can be poured out.
Punishment—the physic that cures the diseases of the soul.
Man—a bartering animal.
Patron—a wretch who supports with insolence, and is paid with flattery.

CHAPTER VII.

DIVISION.

WHAT is Division? Illustrate its rules by examples.

Explain the use of Division in Logic. Give the rules, with examples where they are violated.

What rules should be observed in performing logical Division? Divide—University, Church, Undergraduate, Virtue, Statesman, Science, Art.

Give instances of good and bad Division, showing, in the latter, where the rules are violated.

Another logical process, which is useful for clearness of thought, is division; but this does not, as definition does, point out to us the meaning of a term, but determines *how many* various classes may be contained under one common name: it is 'the exposition of the denotation of a term' (*Fowler*). Thus it is plain that division, together with definition, is exceedingly useful in science for the purpose of classification; the one explains the meaning of a term, the other points out how many various things come under that meaning. Therefore Division should follow Definition, and not come before it, as in the old logic books, for it seems only reasonable to suppose that we cannot divide a thing into its various classes before we know the attributes which belong to those classes separately.

There are three rules set down, as rules for a good division.

1. The dividing members taken separately must contain less than the thing divided.

2. The dividing members when taken together shall be exactly equal to the thing divided; for the whole is equal to all its parts together.

3. The dividing members must be opposed, *i.e.* must not contain each other. There must be but one *fundamentum divisionis* (basis of division).

It is not at all difficult to understand these rules. In the first, the thing divided must always be predicable of the dividing members: *e.g.* if we take 'tree,' and divide it into 'oak, ash, elm,' &c., we can predicate 'tree' of any one of them, thus 'the oak is a tree,' &c.; and so we see that tree is *wider in extent* (as the rule requires) than any of the parts, oak, ash, elm.

The second rule is one which is much more difficult to carry out. All the parts of a term must be enumerated, or included in the division. If, again, we take the term 'tree,' it is impossible to enumerate all the various classes of trees, and the same difficulty will be experienced with many other terms. This difficulty, however, is remedied by a process called Dichotomy by Contradiction, where, *e.g.*, we divide trees into 'oaks' and 'not oaks,' and under the part of the division 'not oaks' all the trees except oaks are included; and therefore, if we add together 'oaks and not oaks,' we have a complete division of the term 'tree' in accordance with the second rule. This division is not at all uncommon. Most readers will be able to recall some one Smith, who divides man thus: into 'J. S. and not J. S.'

The third rule says we must always have the same basis of division. Thus, if we divide 'book,' we must consider it with regard to its size, *or* language, *or* subject; but we must never mix up the three together. Books, as to size, are folio, quarto, octavo, &c.; as to language, English, French, Italian, &c.; as to subject, Historical, Scientific, &c.: but if we divide them into English, Historical, and Folios, we are taking three fundamental divisions, and a *Cross Division*. Divide men into Europeans, Philosophers, Frenchmen, Negroes, and Australians, and we break all the three rules of Division.

INFERENCES.

CHAPTER VIII.

OF INFERENCE.

What do you mean by an Inference? Distinguish Mediate and Immediate Inference.

An inference is the assertion of a proposition gained from a due consideration of another one proposition or more than one other. If such an inference is made from one proposition only, without any use of a middle term, it is called an Immediate Inference, *i.e.* one without a mediate or middle term. Thus, from the proposition, 'All men are mortal,' I am able to assert 'No men are immortal,' and this is called an immediate inference. If, however, a middle term is used in two or more propositions, with which the other terms are compared, and if the inference is drawn in consequence of such comparison, it is a mediate inference. The Syllogism is a good example of this.

'All who are outside the power of fortune are happy.'
'The wise man is outside the power of fortune.'
'The wise man is happy.'

Here the terms 'happy' and 'wise' are each compared with the middle term, which is common to both propositions, and the result of the comparison is the inference 'the wise man is happy.'

Inferences are also Deductive and Inductive. In Induction we argue from particulars to particulars, or to general principles: we take a simple matter of fact, which we have noticed in a particular case, and whenever we find all the same circumstances preceding, we infer that the same event will happen again. But by continued observance, that the same effect follows the same cause, we then may draw a general conclusion, which we keep as a kind of register of our knowledge. Deduction, on the other hand, begins with the general principle, and from it argues to particular conclusions. It will be necessary later on to enter fully into Induction, so that it may be left for the present; and we now examine the various forms of Deductive inference.

CHAPTER IX.

OPPOSITION.

What are the practical advantages of Contradictory over Contrary Opposition? Give examples.

Distinguish Opposition of Terms from Opposition of Propositions.

What are the various forms of Opposition, and which of them has the greatest value, and why? Give examples of each form. State the rules of Opposition, and give examples of Contradictory.

Distinguish Contradictory and Contrary Opposition.

State the relations to each other of Opposition, Conversion and Permutation.

Propositions have already been divided into four kinds, called A, E, I, O, and now, by means of opposi-

Elementary Logic. 31

tion, we shall see how they are related to each other with regard to truth and falsity. Propositions are opposed when they differ in Quantity or Quality, or both: thus they are opposed as Universal to Particular (Subaltern), Affirmative to Negative (Contrary and Sub-contrary), and Universal Affirmative to Particular Negative, Universal Negative to Particular Affirmative, and *vice versâ* (Contradictory).

The student should sit with his face towards the square wall of a room, and in 'his mind's eye' place A in the top left-hand corner, E in the top right-hand corner, and say 'Contraries:' then place I in the left-hand bottom corner, and O in the right-hand, and say 'sub-contraries.' Contradictories will be found to cross from the top left-hand corner to the bottom right-hand, and so on: subalterns will be found on the left and right side. These positions must be learnt by heart; a very little practice will impress them on the memory.

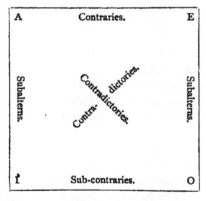

Then the following rules should be learnt.

1. Of *Contradictories*, if one be true the other must be false.

If A is true, O must be false: if I is true, E is false.

2. *Contraries* (A and E) may both be false together, but cannot both be true together. If A is true, E is false: if E is true, A is false. But if A is false, E is unknown; it may be false, or it may be true.

3. *Sub-contraries* (I and O) may be both true together, but cannot be false together. If I is false, O is true: but if I is true, O is unknown.

4. (*A supplementary rule about Subalterns.*) From the truth of the universal, infer the truth of the particular: from the falsity of the particular infer the falsity of the universal.

It will be as well to take one or two simple examples:—

A. 'All men are mortal.' True: O then must be false. 'Some men are not mortal.' By rule 4, E—'no men are mortal'—is false, because O is: I then—'some men are mortal'—is true, because E is false. But E and I are known also from other rules. If A is true, by rule 2, E is false. If A is true, by rule 4, I is true.

Thus if A is true, we know the other three: and by consideration the student will see that if E is true, we know the other three.

Now, take a false example of A.

A. All men are wise. False. Then O is true—'Some men are not wise:' but none of our rules take us farther.

The Sub-contraries are the opposite of the Contraries. If either is false, we know the other three; but if true, we only know that its contradictory is false.

Of the various forms of Opposition, contradictory is the best, because we are by it *quite certain* of the ground on which we base our argument. As may be seen, it is possible for two persons in argument to be false together if they employ Contrary, and true together if they employ Sub-contrary Opposition ; but this can never be the case with Contradictory. Thus we see the use of Opposition : it makes us examine carefully our thoughts and statements, and a neglect of its rules often leads to fallacies, as we shall see further on.[1]

CHAPTER X.

CONVERSION.

IN how many ways may propositions be converted? Illustrate by examples.

What is the object of Conversion, and how is it effected?

Show in what way the Conversion of propositions is affected by the distribution of terms.

State in Logical form and Convert—

There's not a joy the world can give like that it takes away.

Non omnis sapit.

Envious men are disliked.

Fain would I climb but that I fear to fall.

Varium et mutabile semper Fœmina.

Only the honest ultimately prosper.

All cannot receive this saying.

Nemo omnibus horis sapit.

Virtue is a condition of Happiness.

Virtue is the condition of Happiness.

There can be no effect without a cause.

---

[1] The student must practise himself in the rules before given, will be pleased to find that a few performances will make him perfec

I am too late.
Fuimus Troës.
He jests at scars who never felt a wound.
Possunt quia posse videntur.
Pauci læta arva tenemus.
Familiarity breeds contempt.
All things come to an end.
Strong reasons make strong actions.
Man never is but always to be blest.
The better the day, the better the deed.
Evil is wrought by want of thought.
The Spirit does but mean the breath.
All equilateral triangles are equiangular.
Axioms are self-evident.
Diamonds are soluble.
To err is human.
Natives alone can stand the climate of Africa.
He can't be wrong whose life is in the right.
Not one of the Greeks at Thermopylæ escaped.
Some politicians cannot read the signs of the times.
The greatest minds have the least presumption.
Only the ignorant affect to despise knowledge.
Fortune favours fools.
Wherever there is a good conscience, there will be correctness of judgment.
Nothing is expedient which is unjust.
Brevity is the soul of wit.
One touch of nature makes the whole world kin.
All that glitters is not gold.
Raro antecedentem scelestum
 Deseruit pede pœna claudo.

Conversion is a process whereby we transpose the subject and predicate of a proposition. Thus 'Some men

‖ are ‖ wise'—'Some wise things ‖ are ‖ men.' 'No men ‖ are ‖ birds'—'No birds ‖ are ‖ men.' If this is all that we do, the process is called Simple Conversion: and we see by the above examples that the propositions E and I may be simply converted.

If, however, besides simply transposing the subject and predicate, we also are obliged to change the *quantity* of the proposition, it is called Conversion per Accidens, or Conversion by Limitation. This process is necessary for an A proposition: for the great rule to be observed in conversion is this—that *a term must not be distributed in the NEW proposition, which was not distributed in the old.* A distributes its subject, but not its predicate: 'All men ‖ are ‖ mortal' becomes —'mortals are men' by transposing the terms; but as 'mortal' was not taken in its widest sense before, we must not so take it now, and we are constrained to say '*Some* mortals ‖ are ‖ men.' Thus we have changed the quantity of the proposition.[1] An O proposition, as O, cannot be converted, owing to the same rule about the distribution of terms. In converting a proposition we must not change the *quality* of it: O is a negative, and if converted at all must be converted into a negative; and in that case it will distribute its predicate. Example.—'Some men ‖ are not ‖ wise'—'Some wise things ‖ are not ‖ men.' But here 'men' is distributed in the new proposition, when it was not in the old one, and thus the rule is broken.[2] An attempt, however, is made to convert O by what is called Negation. The negative copula becomes an

---

[1] Sir W. Hamilton proposes to *quantify* the predicates, but his system is full of so many and so great intricacies that it is easier to follow the old rules. His plan would reduce all to simple conversion.

[2] Notice how important the rules for the distribution of terms are in conversion.

affirmative, and the negative is tacked on to the predicate, thus :—'Some men ‖ are not ‖ wise'—'Some not-wise things ‖ are ‖ men.' But here we have an I proposition — O is not converted, but was first changed into an I proposition, which breaks the rule that the quantity must not be changed. O cannot be converted at all.

Notice then with regard to the distribution of terms, as influencing conversion, that wherever the terms in a proposition are co-extensive, whether both distributed, as in E, or both not, as in I, such a proposition can be simply converted: but where they are not so, some additional process must take place. In an A proposition the quantity is changed: and it is only in cases where the terms are co-extensive that A admits of simple conversion, as in 'Virtue is the condition of Happiness'—'The condition of Happiness is Virtue.' In an O proposition, as we may not change the quality, no conversion can take place.

Permutation is an inference, where we do change the quality of the proposition. We take the negative of the subject and the predicate for our new proposition: thus

All A is B ∴ No A is not B.
All men are mortal ∴ No men are immortal.

This process is used, as is shown above, for the purpose of converting O: and it depends for its value on contradictory terms excluding each other.

If we add conversion after permutation has taken place, it is called Conversion by Contraposition.[1]

---

[1] See Jevons' 'Logic,' Lesson x.

CHAPTER XI.

SYLLOGISMS.

Define Syllogism and explain your Definition.

Upon what principle do you consider the validity of the Syllogism to depend?

On what principle have the names Major, Middle, and Minor been applied to the terms of a Syllogism? How far are these names generally applicable?

Give and explain the rules which exclude, as invalid, all but eleven out of the sixty-four arithmetically possible Moods.

State the rules of the third figure, and show the reason of them.

Under what circumstances is a Syllogism with two particular premisses valid? Illustrate your answer.

'Distribuas medium.' Does this rule admit of any modification?

Show how it is possible for a valid conclusion to be drawn from particular premisses.

Why is the second figure most convenient for stating a negative argument?

What do you mean by Mood? How many Moods are there, and how many are valid?

'Ex mere particularibus vel ex mere negativis nihil sequitur.' Prove and illustrate the application of this rule to the syllogistic process.

'Sectetur partem conclusio deteriorem.' Illustrate the meaning of this rule by examples.

'*Two particular premisses prove nothing.*' Illustrate by examples.[1]

What Moods are good in the first figure and faulty in the second, and vice versa? Why are they excluded in one figure and not in the other?

How many Figures of Syllogism are there, and how are they determined? Frame a syllogism, E I O in each figure.

Construct syllogisms in A I I in the first figure, and O A O in the third.

Which figure is most convenient:—

1. *For overthrowing an adversary's conclusion.*
2. *For proving a universal truth.*
3. *For establishing a negative conclusion.*

Show that in the second figure only negative conclusions are possible; and in the third figure only particulars.

Give instances of Ferio, Festino, and Baroko, and show why I E O is inadmissible in any figure, A E E in the first, and A E O in the third.

What conclusions can be drawn in the second and third figures respectively? Why do we reject A E E and A O O in the first figure, A A A and E A E in the fourth.

The second figure is that into which negative arguments naturally fall. Explain this statement.

Which of the following Moods are rejected, and why: A A E, A A I, A A O, E O E, I E I, O A O, O I O?

What conclusions can be drawn in the second and third figures respectively?

Show that in a Syllogism an undistributed Middle really involves a fourth term.

Construct arguments involving (1) *an Illicit Major;*

---

[1] These three questions are the same, though differently expressed. They come in almost every other examination alternately in some form or other.

(2) *an Undistributed Middle;* (3) *a Petitio Principii.*
   State and prove the rules of the Second Figure.
   Why is the First Figure called perfect? What is meant by the conclusion following the premises?
   Construct Syllogisms to prove or disprove the following:—

   Trades Unions ought to be made illegal.
   My own College is the best in the University.
   Logic is not a profitable study.
   No woman ought to be admitted to the franchise.
   The law of libel requires to be amended.
   Capital punishment ought to be abolished.
   Royal parks ought not to be used for political meetings.
   Governors of dependencies should be vested with absolute power.
   The proper study of mankind is man.
   Wooden ships will be henceforth useless in warfare.
   Maxima debetur pueris reverentia.

Supply premisses to the following:—
   Cheap bread comes of free trade;
   Therefore cheap bread is an evil.
   Riches beget pride;
   Therefore pride goes before a fall.

Section I.

Of the Nature of Syllogisms.

A syllogism is a mediate inference, where we take two propositions, having one term, the same in each, called the middle term, and by comparing the other terms in the propositions with this middle term, we infer a third proposition; which states whether these terms agree with or differ from each other.

The validity of the process of syllogistic reasoning depends on two Canons, which are stated thus:

1st. *When two terms agree with one and the same third, they agree with each other.* This is much the same as the mathematical axiom: Things which are equal to the same thing are equal to one another.

2nd. When, of two terms, the first differs from the second, and the second agrees with the third, the first differs from the third. These are called respectively the Canon of Affirmative and the Canon of Negative reasoning.

It is easy to see that, if both terms differ from a third, no conclusion can be drawn: for they may agree, or differ *inter se*.

These two Canons apply only to what is called the first figure of the syllogism, and reduce all reasoning to one principle, called the *Dictum de omni et nullo*, which may be stated thus:

'Whatever may be predicated of a term distributed, affirmatively or negatively, may be predicated of everything contained under it.'

In every syllogism, then, there will be three terms, and three propositions. From two of these propositions, which contain a term common to both, the third is inferred, and is called the *Quæstio* or *Conclusion*: the two propositions, from which the Conclusion is drawn, are called the *Premisses*. The three terms are called the *Major*, *Middle*, and *Minor* Terms: and they are so called because in the first figure, which stands thus;

$$B \text{ is in } A,$$
$$C \text{ is in } B,$$
$$\therefore C \text{ is in } A,$$

it is plain that A is the largest of the three terms, and

C is the least, B having a position between each, being less than A, but greater than C. And here it is important to note that the *Major term is always the predicate of the conclusion,* and *the Minor term is always the subject of the conclusion.*[1] The premiss in which the Major term is found is called the *Major Premiss*; that in which the Minor term is found is called the *Minor Premiss*.

Proceeding to find out in how many ways propositions may be formed into syllogisms, we must notice two things: 1st., the Moods, which are the legitimate arrangement of the propositions A, E, I, O, in sets of three; and 2ndly, the Figures, which show the various arrangements of the Middle term with the Major and Minor.

SECTION II.

Moods.

It is possible to arrange the propositions according to Quantity and Quality (A . E . I . O.) in sixty-four different ways, in sets of three. Thus,

```
A    A    A    A    A
A    A    A    A    E
A .  E .  I .  O .  A,
```

and so on. It is advisable for the student to arrange the rest for himself: first taking A, then E, then I, then O: and he will find sixteen of each set—in all, sixty-four moods. But of these, all except eleven are excluded by some one or other of the syllogistic rules, which are stated and discussed below.

---

[1] Bear this well in mind, as it is very useful for what is coming. In whatever form or order the propositions in an argument may be placed, this rule will always assist the student in finding out the proper logical order of the premisses.

Section III.
Syllogistic Rules.

1. *The middle term must be distributed at least once in the premisses.* Here we see the usefulness of the rules for the distribution of terms. A term is distributed when *taken in its widest extent*: so that it is plain that if the middle term is not at least once distributed, it might happen that, though it agreed with each of the other terms, and was common to both propositions, it would not show any connection between the other terms. Thus the premisses,

> All Europeans are men,
> All Americans are men,

do not imply that all 'Europeans are Americans.' 'Men' is not in either case taken in its widest extent, and the example shows that there are some men who are Europeans, and some who are Americans, without their being in any way connected with each other.

But if we say,

> All Europeans are men,
> All Germans are Europeans,

we may rightly infer that all Germans are men.

This rule is very important, and the breach of it leads to numberless fallacies.

2. *If a term is distributed in the conclusion, it must have been distributed in the premisses.* In the words of Aldrich, 'Processus ab extremo non distributo in præmissis, ad idem distributum in conclusione, vitiosus est.' This rule is mere common sense. It is obvious that it would be unfair to take a term in a narrow sense, only including *some* individuals, in the premiss, and then to draw an inference as if it had included all individuals.

This fallacy may be exhibited both with the major and minor terms, and is called an *illicit process*. Thus A E E in the first figure produces an illicit major:

A	All B is A
E	No C is B
E	No C is A.

Now universals distribute their subject only, and negatives their predicate. Thus in the above mood, A E E in the first figure, A is distributed in the conclusion, being the predicate of a negative proposition, whereas it has not been distributed in the major premiss,[1] and thus there is an illicit process of the major term.

Again, E A E, in the third figure, produces an illicit minor:

E	No B is A
A	All B is C
E	No C is A.

Here, C in the conclusion is distributed, being the subject of an universal; but it was not distributed in the minor premiss, as the predicate of an affirmative.

3. *Two negative premisses prove nothing.* It is obvious that if two terms each differ from a third, we can draw no conclusion about them: they may or may not differ from each other. So that two negatives merely assert that there is no connection between the middle and the two extremes.

4. *If one of the premisses is negative, the conclusion must be.* If one of the premisses is negative, the other must be affirmative, and if we assert that the middle term agrees with one of the extremes, and disagrees with the other, we must necessarily conclude that the two ex-

---

[1] It is called the Major premiss, not because it stands first in order, but because it contains the Major term, *i.e.* the predicate of the conclusion.

tremes differ from each other, and such a conclusion is negative.

5. *If the conclusion is negative, one of the premisses must have been negative.* For here the extremes differ from each other: therefore one must agree with the middle, and the other differ from it—in other words one must be affirmative and the other negative.

6. *Two particulars prove nothing.* The only case to discuss is where one is affirmative and the other negative (I O or O I); for we cannot have O O by rule 3, nor I I by rule 1, as no term would be distributed. In O I or I O there is only one term distributed, viz. the predicate of O: this must be reserved for the middle term by rule 1, so that there is no term left to be distributed in the conclusion: but the conclusion, by rule 4, must be negative, because there is a negative premiss, and negatives distribute their predicate. So that in this case there is an illicit process.

Again, in another way, there being no term left to be distributed in the conclusion, it would be an I proposition, as that is the only one which distributes neither of its terms, *i.e.* an affirmative conclusion from a negative premiss, which breaks rule 4.

7. *A particular premiss must be followed by a particular conclusion.* To prove this there are three cases.

1. Let the particular premiss be I, the particular affirmative. The other premiss cannot be O by the last rule: therefore it must be A or E.

Let it be A.   ⎧ All   B is A.
The particular is I. (*Hyp.*)   ⎨ Some C is B.
The conclusion must be I.   ⎩ Some C is A.

For, in A I, only one term is distributed, and this must be used for the middle (rule 1), and thus no

Elementary Logic.

term is left to be distributed in the conclusion: and I is the only proposition which distributes neither of its terms: therefore the conclusion is I, *a particular*.

2. Next, let the universal be E, then the conclusion must be O. Thus,

    E No B is A
    I Some C is B
∴ O Some C is not A.

For E I distribute only two terms, one of which must be used for the middle, and one only is left to be distributed in the conclusion. But the conclusion must be negative, because there is a negative premiss (rule 4); and the negative which distributes only one term is O: therefore the conclusion must be O, *a particular*.

3. Suppose the particular premiss is negative, *i.e.* O, then the conclusion must be O. It must be negative, because one of the premisses is negative (rule 4): we proceed to prove it must be particular. If one premiss is particular, the other must be universal, and as in this case the premiss is particular and negative, the other must be universal and affirmative. Thus

    A All A is B.
    O Some C is not B.
∴ O Some C is not A.

In A O, only two terms are distributed: one must be reserved for the middle, and only one is left to be distributed in the conclusion. But the conclusion must be negative, as one of the premisses is negative, and the negative, which only distributes one term, is O: therefore the conclusion is O, *a particular*.

Therefore, if one premiss is particular, the conclusion must be so too. Q. E. D.

By the application of these rules, all but twelve of the sixty-four moods are excluded. The good ones which remain are

A A A, A A I, A E E, A E O, A I I, A O O,
E A E, E A O, E I O, I A I, I E O, O A O;

and even of these some are excluded, where written in the *figures* of the syllogism.

Section IV.

Figures.

There are four figures under which an argument may be arranged—the figure being the legitimate disposition of the Middle term between the Major and Minor terms. Thus it may be the subject of the Major premiss, and predicate of the Minor (1st figure); predicate of both premisses (2nd figure); subject of both (3rd figure); or predicate of the Major and subject of the Minor (4th figure), thus :—

	1	2	3	4
	B — A	A — B	B — A	A — B
	C — B	C — B	B — C	B — C
∴	C — A	C — A	C — A	C — A.

The fourth figure is said to have been invented by Galen, and is called the Galenian figure.

We are now in a position to test the validity of the twelve moods, which the syllogistic rules have left us, in each of the separate figures. A few examples are given, together with a list of those which are invalid in each figure. It will form a good exercise for the student to try the others himself, and thus test his knowledge of the rules of moods and figures.

Elementary Logic.   47

EXERCISE.

The following Moods are excluded:—
From the first figure, I A I, O A O, A E E, A E O, A O O, I E O:
From the second figure, A A A, A A I, A I I, I A I, I E O, O A O:
From the third figure, A E E, A E O, A O O, I E O, A A A, E A E:
From the fourth figure, A I I, A O O, I E O, O A O, A A A, E A E.
Find out the reason for their exclusion.
Notice I E O is excluded from all the four figures.

In the first   I   Some B is A
               E   No C is B
               O   Some C is not A

Here A is distributed in the conclusion, and it has not been in the premiss; there is therefore an illicit process of the Major term.[1]

Take A O O in the first figure—
     A   All B is A
     O   Some C is not B
     O   Some C is not A.

Here the Middle is distributed: next look at the Major: it is distributed in the conclusion, but not in the premiss. There is an illicit Major.

---

[1] In examining a syllogism, if it is not in logical form, first look for the conclusion and mark the subject and predicate with the proper symbols C and A (or X and Z): then look for the middle term and arrange the argument in its proper figure. After this examine the middle term; if it is undistributed, the argument is invalid; but if the middle is right, go on to the major, the predicate of the conclusion; if this is distributed, look back into the major premiss to see if it has been distributed; if so, all is well; if not so, there is an illicit major; next, if the major is right, examine the minor in the same way.

Take A A A in the third figure,—

    A   All B is A
    A   All B is C
    A   All C is A.

The Middle is distributed: the Major is not distributed in the Conclusion, therefore we need not look back. The Minor is distributed in the Conclusion; look back to the premiss, it is not; therefore there is an illicit Minor.

SECTION V.

Special Rules for Figures.

The following special rules have been made for the four figures; and they will show what kinds of conclusion each figure is best capable of proving:—

Fig. 1. { Minore existente negativa, nihil sequitur.
        { Majore existente particulari, nihil sequitur.

Fig. 2. { Majore existente particulari, nihil sequitur.
        { Ex puris affirmativis, nihil sequitur.
        { In secunda figura semper concluditur negative.

Fig. 3. { Minore existente negativa, nihil sequitur.
        { In tertia figura conclusio debet esse particularis.

Fig. 4. { Quando major est affirmativa, minor semper est universalis.
        { Quando minor est affirmativa, conclusio est semper particularis.
        { In modis negativis, majorem universalem esse oportet.

In fig. 1 the minor must be affirmative by the Canon of Agreement and Difference.

        B — A. Major
        C — B. Minor
        C — A. Conclusion.

If the minor is affirmative, the major must be universal:
for the middle term is not distributed in the minor, and
therefore must be in the major; but the middle is the
subject, and only Universals distribute their subject:
therefore the major must be Universal.

In figure 2,   A — B
                  C — B
                  C — A,

the middle term is the predicate both of the major and
minor premiss, and only negatives distribute their predicate: therefore *one of the premisses must be negative* (2).
If one of the premisses is negative, *the conclusion must
be negative* (3). If the conclusion is negative, the major
term, its predicate, is distributed; therefore it must
previously have been distributed in the major premiss:
but here the major term is subject of the major premiss,
and only universals distribute their subject: therefore
the major premiss must be universal (1). This proves
the three rules of this figure.

In figure 3,   B — A
                  B — C
                  C — A,

the conclusion must be particular. In every syllogism the
premisses must be either both affirmative, or one affirmative and the other negative. In this figure we get both
affirmative and negative conclusions, but they are always
particular. 1st. Let each premiss be affirmative: therefore the terms C and A are both undistributed. But
these are the terms of the conclusion: and the only
proposition that distributes neither of its terms is I, *i.e.*
a particular. 2ndly. Let one premiss be affirmative and
the other negative—the conclusion must be *particular*,

E

though negative. As the conclusion is negative, the major term, being its predicate, is distributed; therefore it must be distributed in the major premiss—this makes the major premiss a negative, as the major term is its predicate: therefore *the minor premiss is affirmative*, and is not distributed: but it is the subject of the conclusion, therefore the conclusion must be particular.

Again, *the minor premiss must be affirmative*. If both are affirmative, obviously the minor is: if one is affirmative, and the other negative, it has been proved above that the major premiss is the negative: therefore the minor is affirmative.

In figure 4,   A — B
B — C
C — A,

when the major premiss is affirmative, the minor must be universal. If the major is affirmative, the middle term is not distributed in it: therefore it must be distributed in the minor premiss, of which it forms the subject: and only universals distribute their subject: therefore the minor must be universal.

2. *If the minor premiss is affirmative, the conclusion must be particular.* If the minor premiss is affirmative, the minor term is not distributed. Therefore it must not be distributed in the conclusion, of which it is the subject: but particulars *only* do not distribute their subject; therefore the conclusion is particular.

3. *In negative moods the major premiss must be universal.* For, in negative moods, the conclusion is negative and the major term, its predicate, is distributed: therefore it must be distributed in the major premiss. But it is the subject of the major premiss, and only universals distribute their subject: therefore the major premiss must be universal.

Section VI.

Syllogism with two Particular Premisses.

Under what circumstances is a syllogism with two particular premisses valid? Illustrate your answer.

      Most men have coats.
      Most men have waistcoats.
∴ Some men have both coats and waistcoats.

Strictly speaking, when each particular premiss is quantified with the word 'some,' two particular premisses prove nothing; but if, as in the above example, the two particulars added together exceed unity, the conclusion is valid.

Take the following example :—

      Most A are B
      Most A are C
∴ Some B are C, and some C are B.

Let A = w, x, y, z.
      w, x, z. are B
      x, y, z. are C:

here it is plain that some B are C, and some C are B. This is a valid conclusion from particular premisses.

Section VII.

Reduction.

On what theory of the nature of Reasoning is Reduction necessary?

Construct syllogisms in Cesare and Disamis, and reduce them to the first figure.

What is the use and object of Reduction?

Reduce to figure 1, *Fesapo, Dimaris, Baroko, Camenes.*

Construct syllogisms in Festino, Bokardo, and Dimaris, and reduce them to the first figure.

Draw up a valid syllogism in the third figure to prove that 'Some changes are useful.' Show the truth of the conclusion both by Ostensive Reduction and Reductio per Impossibile.

Explain the propriety of the term Ostensive as applied to the process of Reduction.

Explain the process of Reductio per Impossibile. For what purpose is it introduced into Logic?

What is the value of Reduction? Reduce Fresison, Disamis, and Festino to the first figure.

'Darii can be reduced per impossibile to Camestres, and thence ostensively to Celarent.' Do this at length: what is the object of the process?

Reduce Darii to Celarent, and Bokardo and Festino to the first figure.

Illustrate by examples the two sorts of Reduction.

Aristotle only considered the first figure to be perfect; the second and third he called imperfect; and he did not, as has been already said, use the fourth figure at all. His principle of reasoning was founded on the 'Dictum de omni et nullo,' which is only applicable to the first figure: and the validity of the syllogisms in the second and third figures depended on their being *reduced* to the first. Thus, on this principle, reduction is necessary. Later logicians have made separate principles for each figure, and with them reduction is impossible. If we apply the laws of Thought, as the principle of syllogistic reasoning, reduction is not wanted at all. Thus the value of reduction depends on what we consider the true principles of Reasoning; its use and object we now proceed to show. The following lines will assist the student to remember the valid moods in each figure, and at the same time convey hints as to the Reduction of the imperfect moods to the first figure:

>Barbara, Celarent, Darii, Ferio*que prioris*:
>Cesare, Camestres, Festino, Baroko, *secundæ*:
>*Tertia* Darapti, Disamis, Datisi, Felapton
>Bokardo, Ferison *habet: Quarta insuper addit*
>Bramantip, Camenes, Dimaris, Fesapo, Fresison.
>*Quinque* Subalterni, *totidem Generalibus orti,*
>*Nomen habent nullum, nec, si bene colligis, usum.*

Of these five *subaltern* Moods, two are in the first figure, A A I, E A O: two in the second E A O, A E O: and one in the fourth A E O. In all these cases a particular conclusion is drawn, where the premisses would justify an universal: these moods, therefore, are a waste of power, and are not of much use. In the first four lines, notice the letters B . C . D . F : the moods in the figures 2, 3, and 4, are to be reduced to those in the first figure which have the same initial as themselves, Datisi to Darii, &c.: the vowels throughout express the mood, Darii = A I I : the letter *s* after a vowel shows that *that* proposition is to be *simply* converted, the letter *p* that it is to be converted *per accidens*: the letter *m* between two vowels shows that the propositions are to be transposed, as premisses: the letter *k* that the mood is to be reduced *per impossible*: the other letters mean nothing.

There are two kinds of reduction which may be applied to all these moods : 1st, *Ostensive*, where we prove in the first figure, by means of the rules of conversic and transposition, either the '*very same* conclusion as before, or one *which implies it*,' e.g.—

D Im	Some	A	is	B	
Ar	All	B	is	C	Fig. 4
Is	Some	C	is	A	

must go to D Ar I I in figure 1. First, the letter *m* tells us to transpose the premisses : we write down

D Ar	All	B	is	C
I	Some	A	is	B,

and we conclude Some A is C, but the letter *s* tells us to simply convert the last proposition, and we get the same conclusion as before.

D Ar	All	B	is	C
I	Some	A	is	B
I	Some	C	is	A.

Again,

F El	No	B	is	A
Ap	All	B	is	C
tOn	Some	C	is not	A,

must be reduced to Ferio in the 1st figure. Here the letters only tell us to convert A *per accidens*, and the syllogism becomes

F Er	No	B	is	A
I	Some	C	is not	A
O	Some	C	is	B.

2nd. The other kind of reduction is called *reductio per impossibile* : in this we prove that our conclusion is true by showing that its contradictory would be false. It is much like the 'reductio ad absurdum' of Euclid, and though it may be used for all the moods, it is chiefly

Elementary Logic. 55

employed for Baroko and Bokardo. Take Baroko, which is in the second figure, and reduce it to Barbara.

B Ar	All A is B
Ok	Some C is not B
O	Some C is not A.

Now, deny the truth of the conclusion; therefore its contradictory is true; and as our first premiss is already A, we leave it, and introduce for the minor the contradictory of the old conclusion, and we have now—

B Ar	∴ All A is B
bAr	All C is A
A	All C is B;

but this conclusion is the contradictory of our former premiss 'Some C is not B,' which was allowed to be true: therefore this new conclusion is false. But it is not false in form, as it is in the first figure: therefore, it must be drawn from a false premiss. But one premiss is the major in the former syllogism, and is allowed to be true: so that the false premiss must be the minor. But this is the contradictory of the old conclusion: therefore the old conclusion is true. Q.E.D.

The process is much the same with Bokardo, as we shall see:

B O k	Some B is not A
Ar	All B is C
dO	Some C is not A.

Here again, we deny the truth of this conclusion, and affirm its contradictory: but here it is the minor, which is universal, so we have

B Ar	All C is A (new premiss)
bAr	All B is C
∴ A	All B is A;

but this is the contradictory of the major premiss in the former syllogism : therefore this conclusion is false. It is not false in form, as it is in the first figure, but must be drawn from a false premiss. Our new premiss, the major, is the false one, and this is the contradictory of the old conclusion : therefore the old conclusion is true. Q . E . D.

CHAPTER XII.

THE ENTHYMEME, SORITES, INDUCTION, ANALOGY, AND EXAMPLE.

Define Example, Enthymeme, and Induction, and illustrate your definition.

Write down some enthymeme in words according to Aldrich, and supply what he considers to be wanting in it.

Explain the Enthymeme. Give instances.

State and criticise Aldrich's view of the Enthymeme.

Inductio est Enthymema quoddam nempe syllogismus in Barbara cujus minor reticetur. Explain and criticise this statement.

In what does the peculiarity of the Enthymeme consist?

Give the rules for the Sorites. Show how they are deduced from the nature of the first figure.

State and account for the limits to the use of a particular, and negative premiss in the Sorites.

State and prove the rules for Sorites.

Give an instance of the argument called Sorites. To ʷʰᵃt logical rules ought it to conform, and why?

Vhat is a Sorites? Give an example. What are the for a Sorites?

Elementary Logic. 57

Give an instance of this form of argument, and break it up into a series of syllogisms.[1]

Estimate the value of analogical reasoning.

Distinguish Induction from Analogy and Example, and give an example of each.

What is Analogy? Give an instance of the argument from Analogy, and state on what circumstances its value depends.

Distinguish between Induction and Exemplum. Can Induction be represented in a Syllogism?

State briefly the nature of Induction. On what principle does it rest?

Aristotle's Enthymeme is a syllogism in *probable* matter, ἐξ εἰκότων ἢ σημείων—from a probable statement, or from a fact supposed to be the *mark* or sign of another fact. The subject is fully discussed in Mansel's Aldrich, Appendix F. An example is there given. 'The εἰκὸς is a proposition nearly, though not quite, *universal*; as "Most men who envy hate:" the σημεῖον is a *singular* Proposition, which however is not regarded as a sign, except relatively to some other Proposition, which it is supposed may be inferred from it.'[2]

Example of εἰκός—

   Most men who envy hate,
   This man envies,
 ∴ This man (probably) hates.

Example of σημεῖον—

   Pittacus is good, (Σ)
   Pittacus is wise,
 ∴ All wise men are good.[3]

---

[1] It will be seen that most of these questions are really the sa' though expressed in different words.

[2] Mansel's Appendix F.   [3] Ibid.

The Enthymeme, as explained by Aldrich and later logicians, is not defined in the same way as the Enthymeme of Aristotle: they define it to be a syllogism with one of its premisses suppressed: sometimes the major, sometimes the minor, as 'All tyrants deserve death: therefore Cæsar was justly killed': the suppressed premiss evidently being ' Cæsar was a tyrant.'

A Sorites is a succession of propositions where the predicate of the first becomes the subject of the next, and so on, till in the conclusion the last predicate is affirmed or denied of the first subject.

    Thus All A is B
          All B is C
          All C is D
          All D is E:
and so on, until All Y is Z
    ∴ All A is Z

This may be expanded into a series of syllogisms in the first figure. It must be noticed that the minor and major premiss are out of the regular order, the minor being written first.[1] Writing them in the proper order, we have

       All B is C
       All A is B
    ∴ All A is C:
       All C is D
       All A is C
    ∴ All A is D:
       All D is E
       All A is D
    ∴ All A is E:

We know it is the minor, because it contains the subject of the con-n, which is always the minor premiss.

and so on, until   All   Y   is   Z
       All   A   is   Y
    ∴   All   A   is   Z.

Rules for Sorites. 1st. *There can only be one particular premiss, which must be the first.*

2nd. *There can only be one negative premiss, which must be the last.*

If these rules are not kept, the special rules of the first figure are broken. In the first figure, the major premiss must be universal: and the minor must be affirmative.

Now, if in the Sorites, any premiss but the first is particular (the first being, as above shown, the minor premiss), there would be a particular major in the first figure, which causes an undistributed middle.

(Minor)   All   A   is   B
(Major)   Some   B   is   C
∴   Some   A   is   C.   Undistributed middle.

Again, if any premiss were negative except the last, it would necessitate a negative conclusion: but in each syllogism the conclusion of one is the minor premiss of the next, and there would then be a negative minor in the first figure, which produces an illicit process of the major term: thus,

(Minor)   All   A   is   B
(Major)   No   B   is   C
∴   No   A   is   C.

(Major)   All   C   is   D
(Minor)   No   A   is   C
∴   No   A   is   D.   Illicit Major.

In a train of reasoning, there are parts called

Pro-syllogism and *Epi-syllogism*: a pro-syllogism is one which supplies a premiss for a new syllogism: an epi-syllogism is one which contains in its premiss the conclusion of a former syllogism.

Induction.

This is one of the great points, where logicians disagree: Material Induction, according to some views, being extra-logical; but, according to others (Mr. Mill particularly), being the only true form of inference. Induction, for the present, may be described as a process of reasoning, where from known particulars we argue to general or universal conclusions, or we take particulars which are known, and draw an inference concerning like particulars which are unknown. In this it is the reverse of Deduction, which starts with Universals, and draws particular conclusions.[1]

Analogy is a kind of Induction, but imperfect, and only a *probable* argument. It has been called the fingerpost of science, as it leads the way to truth. It is an argument from resemblances: when two things are alike in many particulars, and we know that one has a certain attribute, but do not know that the other has, if, in this case we argue, from the similarity of the two things, that the unknown has the same attribute as the known, we are using an analogical argument. Thus Butler, in his *Analogy of Religion*, argues that as there are difficulties in Nature, which we can see, it is probable there will also be difficulties in Religion, both natural and revealed.

The value of analogy depends on the degree of probability which can be adduced. It amounts to a moral

---

[1] On this subject *vide infra*.

certainty that the sun will rise to-morrow : it is almost certain that there will be a frost next January, but the probability is much less that it will freeze on the fifteenth of that month.[1] This is Example, according to Aristotle.

'Example differs from Induction in two principal points. 1. Induction enumerates all the individuals in the minor term, so as to constitute the middle : Example selects single instances. 2. Induction stops at the universal conclusion : Example proceeds to infer syllogistically a conclusion concerning another individual.'[2]

CHAPTER XIII.

COMPLEX OR HYPOTHETICAL SYLLOGISMS.

WHAT is a Complex Syllogism? Give examples of its various kinds.

Give examples of the different kinds of Hypothetical Syllogisms.

Give the Rules for Hypothetical Syllogisms, with instances.

Show that denying the antecedent, or granting the consequent of a Conditional, involves a logical fault, if the argument be expressed in syllogistic form.

State the rules of Hypothetical Syllogisms, and prove them by the laws of Categorical Syllogisms.

---

[1] See Mill's 'Logic,' Book iii. ch. xx.
[2] Mansel's 'Aldrich,' Appendix H.

Explain and give instances of the Conjunctive and Disjunctive Syllogism.

Distinguish between Conjunctive and Disjunctive Hypothetical Syllogisms.

Define Dilemma. Construct a dilemma to prove that 'Examinations are useless,' and rebut it.

State accurately the nature and conditions of a Dilemma. In what different ways may a dilemma be met? Give Examples.

Exemplify the different sorts of Dilemma.

In a former place, Propositions were divided into Categorical and Hypothetical; and hitherto we have discussed Categoricals. A Hypothetical proposition is one in the one part of which some condition is expressed, on the truth or falsity of which the other part depends. The conditional part of the proposition is called the *antecedent*, and the other part the *consequent, e.g.* If A is B, C is D: if A is not B, C is D: if I go out in the rain, I am wet. Propositions of this kind are called *Conjunctive* when the truth of one part depends on the truth of the other; and *Disjunctive*, when the truth of one part depends on the falsity of the other, as 'Either A is B, or C is D:' I shall either go boating or riding: In these cases, if one part is true, the other is false.

Hypothetical Syllogisms are those which are made up of one or more hypothetical or conditional propositions; and they may be either conjunctive or disjunctive Syllogisms. A conjunctive is one where one or both of the premisses is a conjunctive proposition, as—

If A is B, C is D
A is B
∴ C is D.

A Disjunctive is one where one of the premises is a disjunctive proposition, as—

  Either A is B,   or   C is D
     A is   B
  ∴ C is not D.

Both Conjunctive and Disjunctive Syllogisms may be stated in four forms.

 I. Taking the Conjunctive first, we may state it thus

   If A is B, C is D.
    A is B.
   ∴ C is D.

This is called a *Constructive* Conjunctive syllogism, because we assert the antecedent, and here we apply the first rule for hypothetical syllogisms. 'Posita antecedente, recte ponitur consequens :' *Assert the antecedent, and the consequent is true.*

 Another form is this :

   If A is B, C is D
    C is not D
   ∴ A is not B.

This is called the *Destructive* Conjunctive syllogism, because we deny the consequent, and is valid by the second rule : 'Sublata consequente, recte tollitur antecedens :' *Deny the consequent, and the antecedent is also denied.*

 The two other forms are invalid, *e.g.*

If A is B, C is D,   If A is B, C is D
 A is not B,   C is D
∴ C is not D.   ∴ A is B.

These both break the above rules, and if reduced to the form of a Categorical Syllogism, it will be to see where the fault lies. It may be done in this manner:—

Every case of A being B } is { a case of C being D

This is not { a case of A being B

∴ This is not { a case of C being D.

This is A O O in the first figure: 'case of A being B' is the middle term, and is distributed in the A proposition: 'case of C being D' is the major term, and is distributed in the conclusion (being the predicate of a negative), but it has not been distributed in the major premiss: therefore there is an illicit process of the major term. In the other case, where the consequent is affirmed, there is an undistributed middle, which the student may easily find out for himself.

II. The Disjunctive syllogism also admits of being stated in four different ways:—

1. Either A is B, or C is D
    A is B
∴ C is not D.

2. Either A is B, or C is D
    C is D
∴ A is not B.

3. Either A is B, or C is D
    A is not B
∴ C is D.

4. Either A is B, or C is D
    C is not D
∴ A is B.

The Dilemma.

A Dilemma is defined by Mr. Mansel to be 'A syllogism, having a conditional major premiss with more than one antecedent, and a disjunctive minor:' and it is found in three forms. A simple Constructive, a complex Constructive, and complex Destructive.[1]

Thus Ist Simple Constructive, where the consequent is *the same*, but the antecedents *several* in the major premiss.

If A is B, C is D: if E is F, C is D
Either A is B, or E is F
∴ C is D.

Major Premiss.
{ (A is B) (C is
'If the blest in heaven have no desires, they will be
 D) (E is F)
perfectly content: if their desires are gratified, they
 (C is D)
will be perfectly content;

Minor Premiss.
{ But (either A is B)
Either they will have no desires,
 (or E is F)
or they will have them fully gratified;

∴ (C is D.)
They will be perfectly content. (*See* Whately.)

II. Complex Constructive, where *several* antecedents have *different* consequents.

If A is B, C is D : if E is F, G is H ;
But either A is B or E is F
∴ either C is D or G is H.

[1] N.B.—Remember that is *constructive*, where you assert the antecedent; and *destructive*, where you deny the consequent.

F

(A is B)   (C is D)
If I stay in this room, I shall be burnt to death;
(E is F)   (G is H)
if I jump out of the window, I shall break my neck:
(Either A is B) or (E is F).
But I must either stay, or jump out.
(C is D) or (G is H).
∴ I must either be burnt to death, or break my neck.

III. Complex Destructive, where the *several* antecedents have different consequents, which are disjunctively denied.

If A is B, C is D : if E is F, G is H;
But either C is not D, or G is not H.
∴ either A is not B, or E is not F.

'If this man were wise he would not speak irreverently of Scripture in jest; if he were good, he would not do so in earnest; but he does so, either in jest, or earnest; therefore he is either not wise, or not good.' (*Whately.*)

As the alternatives in the dilemma are supposed to exhaust all possible cases, one way of *rebutting* a dilemma is to show that the alternatives are not so exhausted, *i.e.* to deny the minor premiss: as in the case II., I might find a door to the room, unknown to the person who may have locked the known one. If this cannot be done, a dilemma is often retorted by placing the opponent in an equally awkward dilemma.[1] Thus in Aldrich, 'If you marry a beautiful wife, she will be common to all; if an ugly one, she will be a pain to yourself; therefore you should not marry at all'—where the answer is, 'If I marry a beautiful wife, she will not be a pain to me; and if I

[1] See the story of Protagoras and Eualthus (Mr. Fowler's 'Logic').

marry an ugly one, she will not be common to all.' The best answer would be given by showing that a woman might be found neither so beautiful nor so ugly as to cause either difficulty.

The dilemma may be reduced into a syllogistic form, as shown in Whately. 'If Æschines joined in the public rejoicings, he is inconsistent; if he did not join, he is unpatriotic: but he either did or did not join in them; therefore, he is either inconsistent or unpatriotic.' This is reduced thus: 'If Æschines joined, &c., he is inconsistent; he *did* join; therefore he is inconsistent.' And again, 'If Æschines did not join, &c., he is unpatriotic; he *did not* join; therefore he is unpatriotic.' Now an opponent might deny *either* of the minor premisses in the above syllogism, but he could not deny *both*; and therefore he must admit one or other of the conclusions.[1]

CHAPTER XIV.

FALLACIES.

How would you classify the Fallacies? Give instances of the Fallacy of Non causâ pro causâ, and of Ignoratio Elenchi.

Classify the Fallacies. *The most common case of a Formal Fallacy is where there are* four *instead of three terms. Explain this.*

Mention any Fallacies of ordinary occurrence, with instances.

[1] Whately's 'Logic.'

What are the commonest kinds of Fallacies? Give examples of those you mention.

What divisions have been made of Fallacies? Explain, with instances, the Fallacies of Amphibolia, Petitio Principii, Ignoratio Elenchi, Divisio.

Define Fallacy, and explain and illustrate Argument in a Circle, Fallacia Accidentis, A non causâ pro causâ. Compositio. The Fallacy of Achilles.

Define Fallacy, and give examples of Petitio Principii, and Ignoratio Elenchi. Explain, with examples :—

(1) *Argumentum ad hominem.*
(2) *Fallacia plurium interrogantium.*
(3) *Circumstantial Evidence.*
(4) *Arguing in a Circle.*
(5) *Petitio Principii.*

How far does a knowledge of Logic contribute to the detection of Fallacies? Explain and Exemplify (1) *Fallacia Accidentis,* (2) *Petitio Principii,* (3) *Ignoratio Elenchi.*

Construct arguments containing—

(1) *Fallacia compositionis.*
(2) ——— *ignorationis elenchi.*
(3) ——— *consequentis.*[1]

Arguments are either false in *form*, or false in *matter*, and this leads to a division of Fallacies into Fallacies *in dictione* and Fallacies *extra dictionem*. Fallacies *in dictione* are logical fallacies, and are those which have some mistake in the form of the argument, as *e.g.* having four terms and so on. Material fallacies (*extra dictionem*) are those which arise from some falsity in the subject matter, and are not to be discovered without knowledge of the subject, *e.g.* the Fallacy of Achilles and the Tortoise.

[1] Petitio Principii and Ignoratio Elenchi are asked for in five other papers, so should be carefully studied.

Section I.

Fallacies in dictione.

Of the first kind, *i.e.* the purely logical fallacies, are all those which arise from a breach of the syllogistic rules; *i.e.* the fallacy of four terms, undistributed middle, illicit process, two negative or two particular premisses, &c. In addition to these six other fallacies [1] in the form are given, and are called semi-logical.

I. The Fallacy of Equivocation is one in which the same term is used in two different senses: and this is generally the middle term; and in such case the syllogism would really consist of four terms, and is called the *fallacy of the ambiguous middle*. Professor Jevons gives as an instance: He who harms another should be punished: he who communicates an infectious disease to another harms him: therefore, he who communicates an infectious disease to another should be punished. In these sentences the word *harm* is used in two different senses, implying in the first case malice, and in the second negligence.

II. Fallacy of Amphibology. This arises where a sentence is one that is capable of two meanings, not from the double sense of any of the words, but from its admitting of a double *construction*: 'Aio te, Æacida, Romanos vincere posse:' and 'the Duke yet lives that Henry shall depose.' (*Whately.*) In the first case, it is not plain whether the Romans shall conquer Pyrrhus (the descendant of Æacus and King of Epirus), or whether Pyrrhus should conquer them: in the second case it does not say whether Henry shall depose the Duke, or the Duke Henry.

[1] These are the fallacies originally regarded by Aristotle as Fallacies *in dictione*.

III. Fallacy of Figure of Speech. This is closely akin to the two last fallacies, and arises from some peculiar grammatical structure of language. Whately gives as an instance, '*Projectors* are unfit to be trusted; this man has formed a project; therefore he is unfit to be trusted.' Here the sophist proceeds on the hypothesis that he who forms a *project* must be a *projector*; whereas the bad sense that commonly attaches to the latter word is not at all implied in the former.'[1]

IV. The fallacy of Composition, and

V. The fallacy of Division.

In these two fallacies the middle term is used in the one premiss *collectively*, and in the other *distributively*. 'Two and three are odd and even: five is two and three: therefore five is odd and even.' This is a fallacy of Composition: 'Two and three, taken distinctly, are odd and even: two and three, taken collectively, are five:' thus we have four terms, and another case of ambiguous middle. It is the converse of this in Division: the major term is taken collectively, and the minor distributively. 'All the men in this room are thirteen; I am a man in this room: therefore I am thirteen.'

In all these five cases, it is plain to be seen that the fallacy arises from an ambiguous middle, and that there really are four terms in every syllogism which comes under any of these five cases: so that we see that the commonest of all fallacies is that one which has four terms. In addition to these five, there is still another formal fallacy, viz.—

VI. Fallacy of Accent. This also is a fallacy of ambiguity, where it arises from an improper importance being attached to the wrong word of a sentence. 'Thou not bear false witness against thy *neighbour*' im-

---

[1] Logic, bk. iii. § 8.

plies that you may bear false witness against others, but not against your neighbour. The true reading, of course is, 'Thou shalt not bear *false* witness against thy neighbour': it is *false* witness that thou shalt not bear against anyone. The following sentence admits of many meanings, if emphasised on different words: 'The Organum of Bacon is not to be compared with the Organon of Aristotle.' The reader is left to find them out for himself.

SECTION II.
Fallacies extra dictionem.

We now come to fallacies of the other kind, *i.e.* those which are false in the subject matter; these are called Material or Non-logical fallacies, and of them there are seven kinds:—

I. The Fallacy of Accident. This takes place whenever we argue from a general rule to a special case, to which the rule does not actually apply, *e.g.* 'What we buy in the market we eat; we buy raw meat in the market; therefore we eat raw meat.' This is again really a case of ambiguous middle [1]: in the major term we refer to the substance of the meat; in the minor to its condition: the *accident* of rawnesss is added to it.

II. Fallacy *a dicto secundum quid ad dictum simpliciter*. This is the converse of the former fallacy, where the argument is from a special case to a general rule. For instance, we might argue that because some people get killed in the train, therefore we should never travel by rail, or as Professor Jevons states, we are not justified in refusing to give to any particular beggar, because giving 'to beggars promotes mendicancy and causes evil.'

[1] Whately. book iii. § 12.

III. Ignoratio Elenchi. This third form of material fallacy arises from ignorance of the logical laws of opposition, and is called the Fallacy of Irrelevant Conclusion. 'This is the case when the conclusion does not logically follow from the premisses: or when the premisses themselves are not admitted by the opponent; or, when the conclusion, though legitimately deduced from allowed premisses, is an apparent, not a real contradiction of the opponent's position.'[1]

This fallacy occurs chiefly in long speeches, and in many forms; particularly in the *argumentum ad hominem*. 'The hon. member who proposes this measure should not talk about reform; let him look to himself, and see if no reform is needed there.' Here the fallacy consists in the fact of supposing that a man who needed reform in himself could never see or propose any good measure.

Another example of the fallacy may be found in the *argumentum ad populum*, often used by agitators, appealing to the feelings of the people, so that they thereby lose sight of the question at issue. Again, to argue that the result of any measure will be bad; *e.g.* it is all very well in theory but it will not do in practice, is an *ignoratio elenchi*.

Many other examples might be added, but the above are sufficient to assist the student in detecting these fallacies.

IV. Petitio Principii. This fallacy arises in cases where the conclusion has already been assumed in the premisses, or where it is synonymous with one of the premisses, or where one of the premisses is actually proved by the conclusion. The most important form of the fallacy is the Argument in a Circle; and this most commonly arises in speeches, or in books written for

---

[1] Mansel's 'Aldrich.'

proving a special object, or opinion : and is often used without premeditation, for the speaker or author deceives himself as much as his readers. The smaller the circle, the more easy is the fallacy to detect; *e.g.* 'The Scriptures are inspired because they are the word of God : but how do you know they are the word of God ? Because they are inspired.'

'You ought to submit to the opinions of the Prime Minister, because he maintains right opinions. But why are they right opinions? Because they are maintained by the Prime Minister.'

In these cases the fallacy is easy to detect, for the circle is so small ; but in most cases it is difficult to find out where the fallacy lies, owing to the intricate character of the argument.

The best way to detect the fallacy is to narrow the circle, and strip it of all superfluity of words, thus reducing it to a simple and naked form.

It has been said that there is a petitio principii in every syllogism ; that when we say—

>All men are mortal ;
>Smith is a man,
>Therefore Smith is mortal,

we have already asserted the conclusion in our first premiss 'All men are mortal.' The answer is that when we were asserting the general statement, we were not thinking of Smith or any other particular man.[1]

V. The next fallacy we have to examine is called the fallacy *a non causâ pro causâ*, or sometimes *post hoc, ergo propter hoc*. This happens where we argue from a false cause, as : 'There has been a comet, therefore there will

[1] This Theory is discussed in Mill's 'Logic,' book ii. chap. 3, and Mansel's Appendix to 'Aldrich.'

be war;' 'No one ought to drink wine, because it intoxicates': but it is not the wine, but the abuse of it, which is the cause of intoxication. Whately points out that sometimes the *sign* of a thing is set down as its *cause*, *e.g.* 'A great deal of *money* in a country is a pretty sure sign of its wealth, and thence has been often regarded as the cause of it, whereas in truth it is an effect.'

VI. The Fallacy of Too Many Questions. This happens when questions are so asked that no true answer can be given. The example in the old logic books is this: 'Have you left off beating your father?' If you answer 'No,' you imply that you still beat him; if 'Yes,' you imply that you have been beating him. The true answer should be, 'I have neither begun, nor have I left off beating my father.' (See *Aldrich*.)

This fallacy is very commonly resorted to by barristers and others, who desire to make a man commit himself to a double statement.

VII. The fallacy of *non sequitur* is a compound of several of the beforementioned fallacies, and arises where any argument is so loose that it has nothing whatever to do with the premisses: *e.g.* 'The man must have committed the crime, for his father and mother, and all his relations, have been proved to be scamps from their birth.'[1]

Section III.

Exercises on Fallacies.

Examine the following arguments:—

1. If the water in a town is bad, disease will follow; but disease is general; therefore the water is bad.

---

[1] The student is advised, on the subject of fallacies, by no means to neglect a perusal of Whately.

2. It is for the benefit of society that laws should be enforced; criminals are the occasions of laws being enforced; therefore they are public benefactors.

3. None but uneducated persons believe in 'the Claimant.' He is an uneducated person; therefore he believes in 'the Claimant.'

4. Ease of style costs the greatest labour, therefore the easiest style is the most laboured.

5. Dormienti nemo secretum sermonem committit; viro bono autem committit; vir bonus ergo non dormit.

6. Mus syllaba est; mus autem caseum rodit; syllaba ergo caseum rodit.

7. If Herodotus saw all that he relates, he is a credible witness; but much of it he did not see.

8. Pitt was no patriot, for his policy broke down.

9. None but those who claim to possess wisdom can instruct others. As Socrates did not claim the posssession of wisdom, he was but a poor teacher.

10. Nothing is heavier than platina: feathers are heavier than nothing; therefore feathers are heavier than platina.

11. Only warm countries produce wines. Spain is a warm country; therefore Spain produces wines.

12. What we eat grew in the fields. Loaves of bread are what we eat; therefore loaves of bread grew in the fields.

13. When men are pure laws are useless, when men are corrupt laws are broken.

14. The man is on his horse,
The horse is on his legs,
Therefore the man is on his legs.

15. His imbecility of character might have been discerned from his proneness to favourites, for all weak princes have this failing.

16. Nay, look you, I know 'tis true; for his father built a chimney in my father's house, and the bricks are alive at this day to testify it.

17. Quia tu es valde scientificus vir, peto te, ut mihi scribas, quid tu respondere velles ad hunc Syllogismum.

> Asinus habet pedem,
> Tu habes pedem,
> Ergo tu es Asinus.

Ego puto distinguendum inter pedem rationalem et irrationalem.

18. The prisoner is guilty, for the facts of the case are clearly incompatible with his innocence;

19. You can see guilt written in every line of his countenance;

20. Indeed all thieves have certain peculiarities of gait and manner which are discernible in the prisoner, and this is conclusive of his guilt;

21. Many men have been convicted on far slighter evidence, and to acquit the prisoner would be to do an injustice to these men;

22. Finally, his father, mother, and three brothers have been convicted of felony, so that unless you dispute the validity of the Inductive Method, you must convict the remaining member of the family.

23. In moral matters we cannot stand still; therefore he who does not go forward is sure to fall behind.

24. A successful author must be either very industrious or very talented; Gibbon was very industrious, therefore he was not very talented.

25. The end of a thing is its perfection: death is the end of life; therefore death is the perfection of life.

26. The land laws are unjust because the peasantry discontented.

27. Nothing is better than virtue; something is better than nothing; therefore something is better than virtue.

28. Old age is wiser than youth; therefore we must be guided by the decisions of our ancestors.

29. Political assassins ought not to be punished, for they act according to their conscience.

30. This man is wicked, and therefore cannot be happy.

31. Men are not perfect, and therefore are liable to err.

32. All presumptuous men are contemptible; therefore this man is contemptible, since he presumes to believe that his opinions are correct.

33. Italy is a Catholic country and abounds in beggars; therefore France abounds in beggars also.

34. To be acquainted with the guilty is a presumption of guilt; this man is so acquainted; therefore we may presume him to be guilty.

35. The abolition of the Irish Church Establishment is unjust, for it will deprive the Irish Protestants of their religious endowments.

36. Most men have coats; most men have waistcoats; therefore some men have both coats and waistcoats.

37. That which has no parts cannot perish by dissolution. The soul has no parts, and therefore cannot perish by dissolution.

38. The hand touches the pen, and the pen touches the paper, therefore the hand touches the paper.

39. What is universally believed is true; therefore the soul is immortal.

40. Socrates, being a lover of truth, was persecuted; therefore all philosophers are the objects of popular hatred.

41. Cæsar and Pompey both desired to be supreme in the State, and those who desire the same object must be agreed.

42. Poeta nascitur, non fit : why, then, teach verses?

43. They seek revenge, and therefore will not yield.

44. Fuit Ilium : ergo non est.

Suppose that, in an argument on the relative beauty of Gothic and Classical Architecture, it were to be urged—

45. That its very name condemned the Gothic style, as what was Gothic was understood to be barbarous and incongruous.

46. That Classical forms and details were clearly more adapted to puposes of utility.

47. That it was ridiculous in the disputant on the other side to maintain the superiority of the Gothic, when he had built his own house in the other style.

48. That the gradual hold which the Classical style (on account of its greater beauty) was obtaining over the public taste, was enough by itself to prove its superiority.

Draw out clearly the different fallacies contained in these arguments.

How would you meet the following objections to a measure proposed in Parliament?—

49. To pass this measure would be to prefer the wisdom of yesterday to the wisdom of centuries.

50. It calls in question an irrevocable law.

51. If we pass this bill, what further concessions may not be required ?

52. It looks well in theory, but it won't do in practice.

53. Instead of reforming others, let the honourable member look at home and reform himself; he will find enough to do there.

CHAPTER XV.

METHOD.

1. *What do you understand by Method as applied to Syllogisms?*
2. *Distinguish the methods of Synthesis and Analysis.*
3. *Explain* a priori *and* a posteriori.

Method is stated by Aldrich to be such an arrangement of the parts of any discourse that the whole may be the more easily understood (*Talis dispositio partium alicujus disciplinæ ut integra facilius discatur*). But this, according to Mansel, is not sufficiently wide as a definition; for 'Method,' he says, 'has been treated of by Logicians in two principal senses. 1. As a process of inference from the known to the unknown.... 2. As an arrangement of truths already known, with a view of communicating them to others.... Aldrich's definition corresponds only to the second sense of Methodus: but in his subsequent divison he confounds it with the first.' His subsequent division is into

1. Method of Invention or Discovery.
2. Method of Instruction.

But Method, according to the Theory of Formal Logicians, is not a part of Formal Logic at all, as its rules cannot be determined by the Laws of Thought: yet Ramus proposed to introduce it as a fourth part of logic, that it might bear the same relation to Syllogisms as Syllogisms do to Propositions, so that arguments might be arranged in proper form and order. But it is impossible to set down any fixed and determinate rules on such a subject, as the treatment required is so various.

The *method of discovery* is that by which we acquire knowledge, and is employed in induction and inference for the acquisition of general truths from the consideration of particular cases; but *the method of instruction* is that where we use the knowledge thus acquired, or knowledge of general truths not so acquired for the purpose of teaching others. The method of discovery proceeds 'a sensibilibus et singularibus, quæ sunt *nobis notiora*, ad intelligibilia et universalia quæ sunt *notiora naturæ*:' 'from individual objects of sense, and singular cases, *which are better known to us* to things to be comprehended by the intellect, *i.e.* to universals which *are better known in nature*; but the method of instruction proceeds in the opposite way. The method of discovery is that by which almost all scientific inquiries have been determined, *e.g.* in Astronomy, Chemistry, &c.: and these general principles have been *inferred* by Induction: but in Mathematics, as Mr. Mansel shows, 'general truths are discovered by demonstration ; and, till so discovered, cannot, of course, be imparted to others by the method of Instruction.' The former of these methods is also called the Analytical Method, because in it we separate (ἀναλύω) the whole into its parts: the latter is called the Synthetical, because we combine (συντίθημι) the parts into a whole.[1]

This same distinction has been also expressed by the Latin words *a priori* and *a posteriori*. The former is used in reference to knowledge which we gain not by experience ; for some philosophers think that much of our knowledge is innate in us, though not developed ;

---

[1] For a fuller account of Synthesis and Analysis see Mansel's 'Aldrich,' Appendix G.

this is *a priori* knowledge in the strictest sense of the term. This is a knowledge, derived we know not whence, of general truths : but knowledge *a posteriori* is derived from observation and experiment. To argue *a priori* is to argue from premisses known to be true : to argue *a posteriori* is to take a conclusion as true, and to argue backwards to the truth of the premisses.[1]

Finally, it may be said that in most senses the method of Discovery is equivalent to Induction or analysis, or *a posteriori* argument ; and that the method of Instruction is equivalent to Deduction, or Synthesis, or *a priori* argument. It must not, however, be forgotten that arguments, both *a priori* and *a posteriori*, may be applied both to Induction and Deduction : but the most common distinction is the one mentioned here.

[1] The phrase *a priori* has been used in another sense, *vide* Trendelenburg, § 19, note.

INDUCTIVE.

CHAPTER XVI.

INDUCTION.

1. *State the nature of Induction. On what principles does it rest?*
2. *What is meant by the Law of the Uniformity of Nature?*
3. *Contrast* Inductio per enumerationem simplicem *with Scientific Induction.*

Hitherto we have been engaged in examining the rules of Deductive inference, and in a former part of this work a distinction was drawn between Deduction and Induction, which was sufficient for the purpose at the time. It will now be expedient to go on to a more minute investigation of Scientific Induction, and the various processes which belong to it.

Deduction, as we have seen, was a method of arguing from general to particular cases: we are supposed by some philosophers to possess what they call an *intuitive* knowledge of some general laws, or principles, and from them we argue to conclusions which are less general than the original premisses. Those who take this view of the origin of our knowledge would assert that when we say 'All men are mortal,' we do so from something *intuitive* within us, and not from the *experience* we have gained from seeing that individuals die around us. But other philosophers take a different view; they would say that we make the assertion 'All men are ıortal' because we have already observed numerous cases of mortality among men, and that some individuals, whom we have heard of or known, are dead, and we ourselves possess all the same characteristics as these individuals have had, and therefore we shall die ; thus, by Induction, drawing a general conclusion that '*All* men are mortal.' At the same time many who say that much of our knowledge is inductive allow that some of it is intuitive.

In Induction, then, we proceed from the less general proposition to the more general, and gradually establish general principles. Induction, therefore, is the process by which we discover and form general propositions, and refer phenomena, which observation and experiment teach us, to their general laws. If it be true that *all* our knowledge is derived from experience (a point about which there is much dispute), we must see how important a process Induction is : it leads us to those general laws which we store up in our minds as ' registers ;' and then Deduction becomes the process by which we make use of the information we have acquired by the other means.

Induction may be called *Perfect* or *Imperfect*. Perfect Induction is that process in which we are able to enumerate in the premisses all the possible cases to which the conclusion refers; as, for instance, 'that all the months in the year contain less than thirty-two days.'[1] On the other hand, Mr. Mill, who is the authority on Inductive Logic, discusses this in his chapter on 'Inductions improperly so called.'[2] The use of such induction, however, consists in the fact that it enables us to collect our knowledge into some general form, and keep it for use, instead of being obliged from

[1] Jevons.   [2] Book iii. ch. ii.

time to time to go through each separate proposition to prove our conclusion. It is, however, in very few cases that we are thus able to enumerate every single instance to which our conclusion refers : our knowledge at present is too narrow for us to be quite sure that some cases are not left out. Hence it is necessary that we should have some other means of coming to general conclusions. These means we obtain by Imperfect Induction; that is, an induction in which we are not able to enumerate *all* the cases to which our conclusion refers. And this kind of Induction is that which Mr. Mill calls the only true Induction; the other, he says, is of no scientific value whatever. This kind of Induction, therefore, is the one which will be treated of in the following pages.

Induction of this kind may be defined as an inference from *the known to the unknown*, from the present to the absent, not confined to the future, but including also the sum of past experience. It assumes that what is true in one case will be true in another case, if the preceding conditions are the same ; and it is founded on the principles of *the Uniformity of Nature*, and *the Law of Universal Causation* : it assumes that there is order in the Universe, which enables us to maintain, on sufficient degree of evidence, that what has once happened may happen again, if the causes are the same : it investigates the relation of cause and effect; and its validity depends on the supposition that nothing can happen without a cause (which is the law of Universal Causation); and secondly, that the same cause will always produce the same effect (which is grounded on the Law of the Uniformity of Nature).

Here it will be as well to notice that the name of Induction has been applied to other logical processes, which fail in some way or other to come up to our definition of Induction, when we say that it is an inference from the known to the unknown. First, we must distinguish from Induction, as thus defined, another process called *Colligation of Facts*, which consists in our collecting together a quantity of facts in a convenient form, but not inferring anything new from them. But this has its uses and advantages, for it gives us a great grasp over facts so collected, whether true or untrue, and assists us in making further observations and corrections.

The next process which must be distinguished from Scientific Induction is called *Inductio per enumerationem simplicem*, which, according to Bacon, ' *res puerilis est* : ' but at the same time it has a certain logical value, though that value is weak. If we are able to enumerate all the instances, the Induction is then complete, but as it is not an inference from the known to the unknown, it is not the same as Scientific Induction. But if we are not able to enumerate all the instances, the weakness of this Induction consists in the fact that we take no account of any negative instances which might stultify our inference. Any number of positive instances is useless unless we can be quite certain that there are no instances to the contrary, or that, if there were any, we should know them.

In short, if Induction proper is based upon Causation and Uniformity of Nature, and is an inference from the known to the unknown, then *Inductio per simplicem enumerationem* cannot be equivalent to Induction proper ; because it merely enumerates the instances we *know*, and does not proceed any further.

CHAPTER XVII.

DISTINGUISH between Observation and Experiment, and point out the kinds of Induction in which each is most useful.

Inductive Sciences vary considerably in the amount of knowledge they secure, and in the amount of precision with which they secure it. In inductive reasoning we examine Nature, we use phenomena as best we can, and endeavour, by means of Suppositions, Observations and Experiments, to trace effects to their first causes. Most of our knowledge must be founded on experience of some kind; for, according to Bacon, the mind cannot create any new knowledge, entirely independent of Experience. Man is the Servant and Interpreter of Nature. The province of inductive logic is to teach us the methods by means of which we may interpret the ways of nature, and this is done by Observation and Experiment; and the fundamental distinction between these is this: in Observation, we *watch* nature at work; in Experiment, we *make* nature work for us. In the former we regard phenomena *naturally*, in the latter we regard them *artificially*. Observation suggests Experiment, Experiment proves and utilizes Observation: Observation discovers causes by means of their effects, but Experiment helps us to ascertain the effect of a given cause. Thus we see that Experiment stands in a much higher place, and has a much greater practical value in scientific investigation, than Observation has; but at the same time, in some cases, it is impossible to perform experiments, and then we must be satisfied with observation. Experiment is an immense extension of observation, and has many advantages over it; for in experiment we can *vary* the conditions of the phenomena; we can produce them in any degree we choose; we can insulate them from other phenomena; or we can combine them with other phenomena at our discretion. These, then, should be laid down as our rules for proper experiment; we should be careful so to vary, produce, insulate, or combine the phenomena as to give us the greatest possible experience.

But, as said above, there are some cases where it is not in our power to produce the phenomena, and in these cases Observation comes in to our aid. Nature works for us, and we must watch: we cannot make an eclipse of the sun, but by continual observation astronomers have obtained a vast amount of knowledge regarding the character and composition of the sun. Thus we see that in some sciences (astronomy for instance), induction from experiment is impracticable; but those inductive sciences which depend on Observation are very much less valuable than those which depend on Experiment; because, after all, no amount of mere observation can compensate for the scientific value of Experiment. 'Observation, without Experiment (supposing no aid from deduction), can ascertain sequences and coexistences, but cannot prove causation.'[1] On the other hand, Experiment must be accompanied by Observation, for we might experiment all our lives and be none the better for it, if we did not carefully observe effects. And here, too, we must take notice of the caution—

[1] Mill's 'Logic.'

pointed out by Mr. Mill—to discriminate accurately between what we really do observe, and what we only infer from the facts observed. 'To do this well is a rare talent. One person, from inattention, or attending only in the wrong place, overlooks half of what he sees: another sets down much more than he sees, confounding it with what he imagines, or what he infers; another takes note of the *kind* of all the circumstances, but being inexpert in estimating their degree, leaves the quantity of each vague and uncertain ; another sees indeed the whole, but makes such an awkward division of it into parts, throwing things into one mass, which require to be separated, and separating others which might more conveniently be considered as one, that the result is much the same, sometimes even worse, than if no analysis had been attempted at all.'[1]

CHAPTER XVIII.

METHODS OF INDUCTION.

WHAT do you understand by the Law of Universal Causation?

Explain the relation of Cause and Effect.

Name, and distinguish between, the four Inductive Methods.

Which is the more cogent of the Methods of Agreement and Difference?

Give illustrations of the employment of the Methods of Induction.

[1] Mill's 'Logic,' bk. iii. ch. vii.

Elementary Logic.

SECTION I.
Cause and Effect.

The canons of Inductive Logic depend for their validity on the presumption of the Uniformity of Nature, and the invariable order of phenomenal succession, which relates to cause and effect, and may be called the Laws of Causation. This is most essential to inductive inference, because Induction infers from the known to the unknown; and this unknown would be entirely beyond the pale of human presumption even, unless it were made less strange to us by a guaranteed similarity in nature's course. We must find, then, some law or principle underlying the succession of phenomena, which cannot be defeated or suspended by circumstances. Causation produces such a law, and has been divided into Physical and Efficient Cause. The doctrine that efficient causes ultimately produce certain effects is dismissed by Mr. Mill as not belonging to logical enquiry: he recognises only the physical cause, which he defines to be the invariable antecedent with natural sequence. 'The invariable antecedent is termed the cause; the invariable consequent, the effect. And the universality of the law of causation consists in this, that every consequent is connected in this manner with some particular antecedent, or set of antecedents.'[1] Here we must notice that every antecedent is not necessarily the cause of an event, but only that antecedent which is *necessary, or indispensable*, without which there would be no effect at all. Hence we define cause as *the invariable and indispensable antecedent*. Again, there are often more causes than one which produce the effect; and here the consequent is the sum total of the condi-

[1] Mill's 'Logic.'

tions, which produce the effect. The Law of Causation being thus laid down, we can now proceed to describe the inductive Methods.

SECTION II.

The first Method is called by Mr. Mill the Method of Agreement, and the second the Method of Difference. These he calls 'the simplest and most obvious modes of singling out from among the circumstances which precede or follow a phenomenon, those with which it is really connected by an invariable law.'

First Canon. (Method of Agreement.)

If two or more instances of the phenomenon under investigation have only one circumstance in common, the circumstance in which alone all the instances agree is the cause (or effect) of the given phenomenon.

For instance, to follow up Mr. Mill's plan, let A, B, C, D, E, &c., represent the antecedents, and a, b, c, d, e, &c., the consequents: then in the following combination,

```
A  B  C        a  b  c
A  D  E        a  d  e
A  C  D        a  c  d,
```

we notice that A is invariably followed by 'a,' and is therefore according to this method found to be connected with 'a' either as cause or effect. Professor Jevons, in his 'Logic,' illustrates this method by showing the cause of prismatic colours: they depend on the form of the surface of the substance on which they are seen.

But Mr. Mill points out that a difficulty arises in the application of this method, owing to a *plurality of causes*: there may be more causes than one for the same effect. Therefore, in the Method of Agreement, to remedy this defect, we must investigate a great number of instances, which must give us the same result, before we can conclude with any degree of certainty about the connection of the antecedent and consequent in the way of causation.

SECTION III.
Second Canon. (*Method of Difference.*)

If an instance in which the phenomenon under investigation occurs, and an instance in which it does not occur, have every circumstance in common save one, that one occurring only in the former; the circumstances in which alone the two instances differ is the effect, or the cause, or an indispensable part of the cause of the phenomenon.

This method is not liable to the same defect as the former, for in this two instances will prove the point; for example, if we find—

    A B C   produces   a b c
       B C   produces   b c,

we can at once conclude that A and 'a' are connected together in some way of causation. If we know that A is the antecedent, or that 'a' is the consequent, then we know that A is the cause of 'a.' Thus we do not compare instances of the phenomena in which they agree: but we take one case where the instance occurs, and one where it does not, and discover in what way the two phenomena differ. Thus when a man is shot with a bullet, we know that the shot was the cause of his death, for he was in full health immediately before, and if he had not received the shot he would not have died of it. Again, we know that friction is one cause of heat, for if two sticks are rubbed together, heat is produced; if they are not rubbed together, heat is not produced.

Thus by the Method of Difference alone we arrive at

causes, whereas 'the Method of Agreement leads only to laws of phenomena; *i.e.* to uniformities, which either are not laws of causation, or in which the question of causation must for the present remain undecided.' The Method of Agreement, then, is used in most cases where experiment is impossible: but where we can produce our phenomena at pleasure (as Mill points out), the Method of Difference generally affords a more efficacious process, which will ascertain causes as well as mere laws.

Section IV.

Third Canon. (Joint Method of Agreement and Difference.)

If two or more instances in which the phenomenon occurs have only one circumstance in common, while two or more instances in which it does not occur have nothing in common save the absence of that circumstance; the circumstance in which alone the two sets of instances differ is the cause, or the effect, or an indispensable part of the cause of the phenomenon.

This is a double application of the Method of Agreement, where we first take a number of instances where a certain effect is produced, and then a set of different instances where the effect is not produced, *e.g.* if we get various instances where A is followed by 'a,' we have the direct Method of Agreement: and if we could leave out A, and 'a' also disappeared, we should have the direct Method of Difference; but we cannot always do this: but suppose we examined a set of instances where 'a' occurred, and found them to agree in containing A; and then examine a variety of instances where 'a' does not occur and find them agree in not containing A, we

Elementary Logic. 93

have a good proof that A and 'a' are connected together by some fact of causation.

In investigating the cause of double refraction, Mr. Mill takes Iceland spar, and many other substances, which have the power of making things seen through them seem double ; and in all cases they agree in being of a *crystallised* substance ; and by observing that transparent *uncrystallised* substances agree in the absence of this power, the conclusion may be drawn that 'crystalline structure is one of the conditions of double refraction.' The title of this canon is misleading : it is the application of the Method of Agreement twice over, first to positive instances and secondly to negative instances.

SECTION V.

Fourth Canon.   (Method of Residues.)

Subduct from any phenomenon such part as is known by previous inductions to be the effect of certain antecedents, and the residue of the phenomenon is the effect of the remaining antecedents.

If we have a set of phenomena A B C followed by consequents a b c, and we know by previous induction that A B are the cause of a b, by this Method of Residues we conclude that C is the cause of 'c.' The sun and the moon together affect the tides ; if we previously ascertain how much they are influenced by the moon, and subduct it from the influence of both, then it is easy to tell how much is the influence of the sun on the tides.

SECTION VI.

Fifth Canon.   (Method of Concomitant Variations.)

Whatever phenomenon varies in any manner, whenever another phenomenon varies in some particular man-

ner, is either a cause or an effect of that phenomenon, or is connected with it through some fact of causation.

This method is the one used for what are called Permanent causes, or indestructible natural agents, such as the earth, air, heat, the sun, &c. It is impossible with these to employ any of the methods we have already discussed, because it is impossible either to exclude or isolate them; and we can neither hinder them from being present nor contrive that they shall be present alone. But we may produce, or nature may produce for us, some modification or variation of the antecedent. If we have three antecedents A B C followed by a b c, and we notice that whenever A varies the consequent 'a' also varies, 'b' and 'c' remaining the same, we can infer that A and 'a' are connected together by some fact of causation. One of the simplest cases is the variation of the tides in consequence of the variation of the moon. It has also lately been discovered that the Aurora Borealis is accompanied with magnetic storms, and also the appearance of larger spots than usual on the Sun. These may be connected through some fact of causation.

CHAPTER XIX.

DESCRIBE the nature and use of Hypothesis.
Distinguish Hypothesis and Empirical Law.
How may a valid be distinguished from an invalid Hypothesis?

Hypothesis is derived from the Greek words ὑπὸ and τίθημι, to place under, and is equivalent to the Latin word *suppositio*; it is a supposition suggested with more or less plausibility to account for a certain number of phenomena which we observe, but which we cannot explain scientifically. Scientific explanation means the resolving a uniformity, which is not a law of causation, into the laws of causation from which it results, or a complex law into simpler laws. If *beneath* these phenomena we can *place* some sufficient reason why they exist together, or why they accompany each other, we are said to refer them to their origin, or scientifically to trace cause and effect. But we are not always able to do this offhand, so that we have to start many hypotheses which may not always even be true; for true theories are often preceded by false ones. For instance, the theory of planetary motion, namely that the planets moved in circles, was false, and Kepler himself is said to have started nineteen false theories before he hit upon the true one, namely, that the course of the planets is elliptical.

The same thing happens in almost all branches of science.

I. Hypothesis must never be confounded with proof, but one point in which it is serviceable is to lead the way to proof; for sometimes even a hypothesis, false in itself, will suggest a true one, as we have seen in Kepler's case. But the truth of the hypothesis depends on subsequent verification : hence we get one rule for hypothesis, that *it must be capable of proof or disproof.* For imagination or fancy is the parent of hypothesis, and if we had not some such rule as this, there would be no end to the fanciful suppositions that might be started.[1]

II. Another use of hypothesis, if it can be applied to *all* the known facts, is to bind them together, and bring them under one point of view. Hence we get a second rule, that *the hypothesis must be adequate to the ex-*

[1] For instances which break this rule, see Prof. Fowler's 'Inductive Logic.'

planation of all the observed phenomena. The instance of inadequate hypothesis made by Voltaire, that 'the marine shells found on the tops of mountains are Eastern species, dropped from the hats of pilgrims, as they returned from the Holy Land,'[1] is amusing; for it does not account for the number of the shells, or for their being found far from the tracks of pilgrims, or for many of them not being Eastern at all.

III. Again, hypothesis *must be consistent with the laws of thought*, and must not be known, or even suspected to be untrue, for it would be manifestly absurd to endeavour to discover truth from what is known to be false beforehand. The validity of hypothesis, then, depends on the observance of these three rules, and if they are duly observed the hypothesis is called legitimate.

Now that we have investigated the nature of hypothesis, it will be easy to distinguish it from an Empirical Law. 'Scientific enquirers,' says Mr. Mill, 'give the name of empirical laws to uniformities which observation or experiment has shown to exist, but on which they hesitate to rely in cases varying much from those which have been actually observed, for want of seeing any reason *why* such a law should exist.'

We see, then, that the difference consists in this: hypothesis refers to a law *supposed* to exist; empirical law is one *known* to exist, though the reason of it is not understood. The following are instances of empirical laws: that certain changes of the weather are indicated by certain appearances in the sky; that after the fusion of metals, the alloy is harder than the elements; and many others; all of which are known to be true from repeated observation, but cannot be resolved into simpler laws, which would give the reason for them.

[1] Fowler.

CHAPTER XX.

PROBABLE REASONING.

ALL knowledge searches after truth ; and as all knowledge differs in kind, so also must it differ in the degree of its truth. An important part of inductive knowledge, not having attained to what is universal and uniform, only amounts to an approximation to such truth. Conclusions which rest on probable evidence are drawn from approximate generalisation, and there is no reason why the degree of the knowledge we have attained should not deserve reliance, although unable to conform to the more precise accuracy of logical uniformity. Nowhere more than in Social Science and in Politics are we compelled to utilise probable evidence, and approximate generalisations. When sufficient Induction has not occurred, we cannot make a general law for the purpose of deduction; and as the complexity of social phenomena cannot be easily deciphered, nor can results be prescribed with exact assurance, we must therefore be content with probable evidence. Probability upon Probability can so strengthen modified Premisses as finally to make the conclusion sufficiently sure, morally certain; and this is the nature of Circumstantial Evidence. Probable arguments may be combined together, as so many links in a chain, each concentrating upon the same conclusion, and the accumulative testimony of so many in-stances is often in exact proportion to their nur value. But the comparative value of circumstantial evidence must always be tested by the strength or weakness of counteracting testimony. Logic and common sense would alike ignore a negative fraction contrasted with a positive unit; but if the multiplication of independent testimony points directly to the same conclusion, that conclusion must be valid, and the moral certainty it thus establishes must amount to scientific truth.

The only danger of these conclusions is, that they are often the approved result of violent presumption, and all probable arguments, especially circumstantial evidence, are only too liable to overlook negative instances and 'the benefit of the doubt.'

The value of Circumstantial Evidence is this, that its strength is often in weak and trivial details, which in accumulative testimony furnish Positive Proof. In great matters Direct Evidence often breaks down, owing to Misrepresentation, Delusion, or wilful Perjury; the point blank oath of isolated testimony is not such reliable moral certainty as the striking convergence of numerous circumstances, and the striking concord of numerous tests.

Circumstantial Evidence may therefore be defined as a series of probable circumstances, accumulated together, and tending towards the same conclusion. But only when we have fairly exhausted every supposition for and against, must we cautiously strike the balance in favour of such Presumptive Evidence.

INDEX.

[The figures refer to the pages of the book.]

ABSOLUTE TERMS, or non relative, 9
ABSTRACT TERMS, 9
ACCENT, fallacy of, 70
ACCIDENT, a predicable, 22, 23; a fallacy, 71
ACCIDENTAL DEFINITION, or description, 25
A DICTO SECUNDUM QUID, &c., a fallacy, 71
ADJECTIVE, syncategorematic words, 8
AFFIRMATIVE PROPOSITIONS, 15
AMBIGUITY, fallacy arising from 69
AMBIGUOUS, or equivocal terms, 9
AMPHIBOLOGY, fallacy of, 69
ANALOGOUS TERMS, 9
ANALOGY, 60
ANTECEDENT, part of a conditional proposition, 62
A POSTERIORI KNOWLEDGE, 80
A PRIORI KNOWLEDGE, 80
ARBOR PORPHYRIANA, 12
ARGUMENT, syllogistic, 39
ARGUMENTUM AD HOMINEM,
,, AD JUDICIUM,
,, AD IGNORANTIAM,
,, AD POPULUM,
',, AD VERECUNDIAM, forms of the fallacy of Ignoratio Elenchi, 72
ART AND SCIENCE, Logic both, 3–5
ASSERTION, an affirmation or denial, 15–17

ATTRIBUTIVE TERM, i.e. connotative, 11

BABARA, a mood of the syllogism (*see* Mood), 41
BEGGING THE QUESTION, fallacy of Petitio Principii, 72

CANONS OF SYLLOGISM, affirmative and negative, 40
CANONS OF MILL'S INDUCTIVE METHODS—
1. Method of Agreement, 90
2. ,, ,, Difference, 91
3. Joint Method, 92
4. Method of Residues, 93
5. ,, ,, Concomitant variations, 93
CATEGOREMATIC WORDS, those which may be employed by themselves as terms, 7
CATEGORICAL PROPOSITIONS, those which assert or deny absolutely, 15
CAUSE, meaning of, 89
CIRCLE, argument in a; a form of Petitio Principii, 72
CLEARNESS OF KNOWLEDGE, Logic conduces to, 5
COLLIGATION OF FACTS no new inference, 85
COLLECTIVE terms, 8
COMMON terms, 8
COMPLEX CONCEPTION, a term

COM

which consists of many words, 8
COMPLEX OR HYPOTHETICAL SYLLOGISMS, 62
COMPOSITION, fallacy of, 70
COMPREHENSION of Terms (*see* Connotation)
CONCEPT, 5
CONCRETE terms, 8
CONDITIONAL propositions, 62
CONNOTATION of terms, 11
CONSEQUENT, the part of a conditional proposition which depends on the other, 62
CONSTRUCTIVE Syllogism, 63
,, Dilemma, 65
CONTRADICTION, a form of opposition, 31
CONTRADICTORY terms, 9
CONTRARY terms, 9
CONTRAPOSITION, a form of conversion, 36
CONVERSE FALLACY of Accident, a dicto secundum quid ad dictum simpliciter, 71
CONVERSION, 35
— questions on, 33
COPULA, the connecting link between the subject and predicate of a proposition, 14
CORRECTION of observations, 88
CROSS DIVISION, 28

DEDUCTION, a form of inference, 30
— distinguished from induction, 82
DEFINITION, 24–26
DENOTATION of a term, also called extension, 11
DESCRIPTION, an imperfect definition, 25
DESTRUCTIVE SYLLOGISM, 63
DICHOTOMY, a form of division, 28
DICTUM DE OMNI ET NULLO, 40
DIFFERENCE, a predicable, 22
DILEMMA, 65–67
DISCOURSE or reasoning, otherwise Syllogism, 39, 40
DISJUNCTIVE Proposition, 62
,, Syllogism, 64
DISTRIBUTION of terms, 19
DIVISION, principle and rules of, 27
— by Dichotomy, 28

IGN

DIVISION, Cross Division, 28
— place in Logic, 27

EMPIRICAL LAW, 96
— — distinguished from Hypothesis, 96
ENTHYMENE OF ARISTOTLE, 57
— as explained by Aldrich, 58
EPISYLLOGISM, 60
EQUIVOCAL terms, 9
— — fallacy of, 69
ESSENTIAL PROPOSITIONS, otherwise Verbal, 16
EVIDENCE, circumstantial, 97, 98
EXAMPLE, 61
EXPERIMENT as distinguished from Observation, 86-88
EXPLANATION, meaning of, 95
EXTENSION of a term, otherwise Denotation, 11

FALLACIES in dictione, 69, 70
— extra dictionem, 71–74
— exercises on, 74–78
FALSE CAUSE, fallacy of, 73
FIGURE OF SPEECH, fallacy of, 69
FIGURES OF THE SYLLOGISM, 46
— exercises on, 47
— special rules of, 48
— special rules proved, 49, 50
FUNDAMENTUM DIVISIONIS, a rule of division, 27

GALENIAN FIGURE, the fourth figure of the syllogism, 46
GENUS, one of the Predicables, 21
,, Summum, 21
GRAMMAR, how different from Logic, 3

HEADS OF PREDICABLES, 21
HYPOTHESIS, nature and rules of, 95, 96
HYPOTHETICAL SYLLOGISMS, 62–64

IGNORATIO ELENCHI, the Fallacy of Irrelevancy, 72

Index.

ILLATIVE CONVERSION, that of E and I propositions, 35
ILLICIT PROCESS, 42
— — of Major term, 43
— — of Minor term, 43
— — a fallacy, 69
IMAGINATION, as distinguished from perception, 4
IMMEDIATE INFERENCE, 29
— — by opposition, 30
— — by conversion, 33
IMPERFECT INDUCTION, 83
INDEFINITE propositions, 16
INDUCTION, 60, 82
— distinguished from deduction, 29, 82
— methods of, 88–94
— perfect or imperfect, 83
— 'per enumerationem simplicem,' 85
INFERENCE,—
— Definition, 29
— Mediate, 29, 39
— Immediate, 29, 30, 35
— Deductive ⎱ 29, 82
— Inductive ⎰
INFIMA SPECIES, 21
INSEPARABLE ACCIDENTS of a class and of an individual, 23
INTENSION, otherwise Connotation, of a term, 12
IRRELEVANCY, fallacy of, or ignoratio elenchi, 72

JUDGMENT, called by others Proposition, 5

LANGUAGE, use of, in Logic, 3
LOGIC, definitions by various writers, (Whately, Mill, Mansel), 2
— its province, 2
— its relation to psychology, 1
— distinct from Grammar, 3
— ,, ,, Rhetoric, 4
— its use, 5, 6

MAJOR AND MINOR term defined, 40
,, ,, Premiss, 41
METHOD, 79

MIDDLE TERM, 40
— — ambiguous, 69
MNEMONIC VERSES, &c., for use in reduction, 53
MODALITY not expressed by the Copula, 15
MOODS 41, determined by rules of Syllogism, 42–45
— exercises on, 47
— subaltern, 53

OPPOSITION of terms, 9
— of propositions, 30
OSTENSIVE REDUCTION, 53

PARONYMOUS terms v. fallacy of figure of speech, 69
PERCEPTION, 4
POSITIVE terms, 8
PREDICABLES, heads of, 21
PREDICATE of a proposition, 15
— its relation to the subject, 21–23
PREMISSES, 40
— Major and Minor, 41
— Negative, 43
— Particular, 44, 51
PRINCIPLE OF DIVISION, or Fundamentum Divisions, 27
PROBABLE REASONING, 97
PROPERTY, 22
— Mills' definition of, 22
PROPOSITION, definition of, 14
— division of, 15
— complex or hypothetical, 62
— verbal and real, 16
PROSYLLOGISM, 60
PSYCHOLOGY, 1

QUALITY OF PROPOSITIONS, 15
QUANTITY OF PROPOSITIONS, 16
QUANTIFICATION of the predicate, 17

REDUCTION, 52
— Ostensive, 53
— per impossibile or ad absurdam, 54
— of hypothetical syllogisms, 64

Index.

SEC
- SECOND INTENTION, term of, 10
- SEPARABLE ACCIDENT, 23
- SINGULAR terms, 8
- — propositions used as Universals, 16
- SORITES, definition of, 58
- — rules for, 59
- SPECIAL RULES for the figures of a syllogism, 48
- — — the same proved, 49, 50
- SPECIES, 21
- SUBALTERN genera and species, 21
- — moods, 53
- — opposition, 31
- SUBJECT of a proposition, 15
- SYLLOGISM, nature of, 39
- — moods of, 41
- — figures of, 46
- — canons of, 40
- SYLLOGISMS, complex, 62
- SYLLOGISTIC Rules, 42

VER
- SYNCATEGOREMATIC WORDS, 7
- SYNTHETIC JUDGMENTS, otherwise Real Propositions, 17
- TERMS, various kinds of, 7-10
- — connotation and denotation of, 11-13
- — distribution of, 19
- — opposition of, 9.
- THOUGHT, its relation to langu 3
- — products of, 5
- UNDISTRIBUTED MIDDLE, fallacy of, 42
- UNIVOCAL terms, 9
- VERBAL propositions, 16

Lightning Source UK Ltd.
Milton Keynes UK
UKHW012012090322
399819UK00002B/381